ON THE MONASTIC LIFE

By: H.H. Pope Shenouda III

ON THE MONASTIC LIFE

~ By: H.H. Pope Shenouda III ~

ST SHENOUDA'S MONASTERY
SYDNEY, AUSTRALIA
2016

On the Monastic Life

ST SHENOUDA MONASTERY
8419 Putty Rd,
Putty, NSW, 2330
Sydney, Australia

www.stshenoudamonastery.org.au

ISBN 13: 978-0-9945710-0-7

Contents

The Right Aim   7

Healthy Monastic Life   15

The Readings During The Consecration of A Monk   33

God's Promises To The Monk   51

Monks Are Earthly Angels   63

The Work of God In The Life of A Monk   71

Monastic Life Is Different To Worldly Life   85

Monastic Rules   103

Life of Continuous Prayer   125

Balance   135

The Life of Discipline   147

Seriousness In The Spiritual Life   157

The Remembrance of Evil Entailing Death   165

Routine   173

The Inner Work   183

A Life of Struggle   193

Time for A Monk   203

Asceticism In Monasticism   213

Quietness In Monasticism   221

Questions & Answers   235

THE RIGHT AIM

St. Isaac says the following about monastic life and silence, "There are three things, which a person who lives in tranquillity needs: an honourable target, completing their canon and remaining quiet."

The right aim in monasticism is very important. This aim dictates the life of a monk. Why has a monk abandoned the world and joined a monastery? The only target is the love of God and that is why a monk abandons the world. If he has another target, then it is not a correct one. In the Holy Liturgy we say, "they lived in the mountains, wilderness and the holes of the earth for the sake of their tremendous love for Christ the King". A person loves God so much and wants to worship God deeply, thus he leaves the world.

The means then should be appropriate to the target. A monk who does not put these three important things before his eyes when coming to the monastery is mistaken. It is something to be practised before entering the monastery; either the life of solitude, serenity and calmness, or the life of service. He should also practise the life of purity of the heart, living a life of repentance, and growing in various virtues.

If a person wants to build himself solely as a result of joining monasticism, the result will be that he will lose himself and others around him. He will become a selfish person and will not be able to deal with the brethren in the monastery.

The life of a monk in the monastery is based on three things: solitude, service, and purity of heart. If a monk desires a pure heart, it will not matter whether he lives in solitude or in the community. He will only be focused on keeping his heart pure, communicating with people to discover his faults and to correct them. He will be keen to have the blessing of everyone through obedience and submission, placing everyone above himself as St. Anthony said, 'Let everyone bless you.' Such a monk targets purity of heart.

As we have already mentioned, the target is the love of God. If someone's target is worship and continuous prayer, he would say, "I need to live alone. I cannot achieve this while living with others." Actually, no one can live in solitude to worship unless he has achieved purity of heart. Thus purity of the heart comes first and then worship; lest worship not be accepted.

Some monks think that they are not considered monks unless they grow in physical virtues related to the body, such as fasting. They target a special level of asceticism in fasting and abstaining, maybe for several days. They refrain from certain foods for an entire lifetime, even in feasts, and fast until sunset.

Monks might think that monasticism is the ascetic clothing, simple dwelling, and living in poverty. Also monks may think that monasticism is seen virtues, while forgetting the inner work of purity of heart. A monk may focus only on the certain number of prostrations to perform, or reaching a certain level of fasting. He does not care about the status of his heart; is it humble, meek, tolerant, pure and loving? They may even lose love for other people or criticise others for not fasting like them, asking about the number of their prostrations and comparing.

Truly, if a person wants to live according to an honourable target, which corresponds with the love of God, he has to acquire the virtue of purity of heart. He should also acquire the life of; repentance, humility, meekness, tolerance, serenity. The person aims to have everyone's blessings and love, serving everyone. It is only then he starts withdrawing from people bit by bit, through guidance, until he completes the life of worship, prayer and solitude according to God's will.

The target which a person specifies for himself will determine his behaviour. An example is knowledge; which kind of knowledge is a monk keen to know. For some it is the Holy Bible and its meditation, for another it is the spiritual or theological books. Yet for another it is the ascetic books talking about monastic life.

If someone is intending on the solitary life, he should read the books of St. Isaac, St. John of Assiut and the Philokalia. If someone is targeting service, he should read theological and doctrinal books, and all religious knowledge about rites, doctrine, theology, language... etc.

If purity of the heart is one's target, he will read spiritual books about that topic and try to apply and concentrate on spiritual practices more than the spiritual readings. It is important then that a person should have a clear target and means, making sure that he is progressing daily towards this target. If he does not have a clear target he will live haphazardly without control of his deeds. He might even wonder if he is progressing or not. He might ask himself why did I join a monastery, or what is the benefit of being a monk, falling into many doubts?

If your target is not clear or honourable, at least aim to give an account of yourself, asking why did I leave the world and come here? What is monasticism? Am I living like a monk or not? Am I progressing in my monasticism, or even going back?

For sure out of humility one would say they are nothing. If a monk was to evaluate his life and be on the right path, he would find that it is because of the grace of God, and this would help him from falling into vain glory. In this case he should also compare himself to the supreme ideal examples of monasticism, saying within himself, 'yes, I am living according to the correct path but still there is a long way to go, and I have achieved nothing of it.' He should give a self-account thoroughly.

Whether the monk is living the life of solitude, service or worship he needs purity of the heart. Every person's target should be the purity of the heart. It is the first step in the monastic life, without it worship is not accepted.

There are unacceptable prayers, "The sacrifice of

the wicked is an abomination to the Lord." (Prov.15: 8). God did not accept the prayer of the Pharisee, or those of whom He said, "When you spread out your hands, I will hide My eyes from you; even though you make many prayers, I will not hear." (Is 1: 15). For our prayers and fasting to be accepted they have to come out of a pure heart, as the Lord says, "Is it a fast that I have chosen?" (Is. 58: 5).

If the life of solitude is not preceded by purity of heart, it will be in vain. This will change from the goal of worshipping God to escaping and dealing with people. One of the fathers said: "There is a person who might sit 50 years in the cell without knowing how to sit in the cell."

Thus, the number one thing in our lives should be the purity of the heart. It is in need of a good examination of one's self, discovering and curing our mistakes.

Unfortunately, we may sometimes find problems in the monastic life between monks. This happens in the world because people living in the world all have different targets, means, religions, beliefs, principles, values...etc. In monasticism however, we find a number of people who have left the world for one target. They live in one house, eat at one table, and pray in one church. They are brothers in a small group who have gathered together for their love of God. We can even say that they are an ascetic group who have died to the world; they believe in all virtues and agree on certain values. Hence if this small group, who have agreed on one target, living in worship and asceticism, cannot cooperate with each other, it is a very dangerous issue and following God becomes difficult. If the saints cannot deal with each other, what about the people of the world? "If therefore the light that is in you is darkness, how great is that darkness!" (Matt 6: 23).

How can such things as fights, anger, conflicting desires and arguments be present in such a small group who cannot deal with each other? They may criticise each other, forming a sub-group and so on. Truly this is a very unfortunate issue.

Some would say that purity of heart is their number one goal, yet others may be falling short. The reason that purity of heart is not a priority in some is possibly because the person is suffering from pride from within. They do not confess their mistakes hence they are not amended. Therefore, to reach purity of the heart, we must discover our faults and try to cure them by confessing. If we keep finding excuses for our faults and don't confess that we have done something wrong, we will never reach purity of the heart.

To attain purity of heart, a person should examine himself honestly, and only judge himself.

One of the most difficult things in monastic life arises from the monks who spoil themselves. They also want others to spoil them. When we say 'spoil' we mean when a person is so sensitive about his personal dignity. He wants everyone to honour him and treat him in a special way. His wishes become orders and he gets angry quickly and complains if they are not carried out immediately. He adds to any bitter soul more bitterness, forgetting all about humility, tolerance and dying to the world.

However a person who does not spoil himself, preferring to be strict, and desires to win victory over himself, will be honest and admit his weaknesses to reach a pure heart. Once one starts to do this he will become a true monk.

I think if it happens that anyone loses his peace in monasticism, it would arise from a non-monastic reason. There is no monastic reason which could lead a person to lose their peace. Monks are earthly angels, do angels lose their peace? Do angels become angry? If so they are not angels anymore.

Healthy Monastic Life

The Target:

Firstly, the monk should have an appropriate target for joining monasticism. If not, he should at least correct his target after joining monasticism. In monasticism, the proper target is to consecrate our time to sit with God and abide in His love. The original healthy aim of monasticism is the life of silence, solitude, prayer, and repentance.

It is a common thought that development in monasticism is just development in the life of solitude. One person moves from living in community to living as a solitary in the monastery. Actually that is not the only target in monasticism; there are other targets such as the purity of the heart. A person may be living in solitude, yet has not reached purity of the heart.

In the history of monasticism we find fathers who excelled in the virtue of silence and repentant tears such as St. Arsanius and St. Moses the Black. Others excelled in the virtue of humility and endurance, such as St. Anna Simone. Others in the virtue of continuous prayer such as St. Makarious of Alexandria and many hermit fathers. Each one chose a virtue and did their best to grow in it.

It was said about St. Bishoy that once he excelled in a virtue and people began knowing about it, he would move to another virtue so that his virtues might not be disclosed to people. The most important thing is that monasticism for these saints was the life of virtue in general and the purity of the heart from within.

A person whose mistakes are disclosed to him will begin removing them one after the other until they have all been cast away. This is why monasticism is called the life of repentance. A person who knows his mistakes and corrects them one after the other is living the life of repentance. He is never upset if anyone rebukes him, but rather rejoices that his accuser is disclosing his mistakes to him so that he might correct himself.

Those that lived the life of repentance in monasticism also had the virtue of weeping for their sins. Their hearts were sensitive with running tears. There are special tears for repentance as it is said, 'Sit in your cell and weep for your sins.' Which one of us would have the target of sitting in his cells and weeping for his sins?

One of the prominent monks in the life of repentance in monasticism was Anba Shishoy, sometimes called 'Sisoy'. He lived in the eastern desert on St. Anthony's mountain. Even during the departure of his soul he was asking for another chance to repent.

Thus the inner aims of monasticism are repentance, purity of heart, and discovering one's weaknesses in order to improve. Such people do not get annoyed from rebuke but rather rejoice. They are truly humble having the gift of tears, considering everyone more righteous, better and stronger than themselves. Thus the life of repentance gives them humility. Anger is always accompanied by pride of the heart because that pride inside the heart arouses anger to protect dignity.

A repentant person is truly humble. They consider themselves worse than that which is told to them. During the ordination of St. Moses the Black he was dismissed by Pope Theophilus. Thus he said to himself, "You deserve it, O black coloured. You are not among humans. Why are you standing among people?" He rebuked himself. He did not get upset with those who dismissed him, although they were the ones who had invited him.

Monasticism and Solitude:

Solitude is not the sole aim of monasticism, and it is in vain without repentance. It does not lead to the Kingdom of God like repentance. Yet if both solitude and repentance are combined together it is a fortification.

Life among the brethren is more helpful for the life of repentance. How? There was a monk who went to an elder monk and said to him, "I am living in leisure and there are many sins which do not bother me." So the elder answered, "My son, that is because you are living as a solitary and there are no fights with others. Yet go to the monastery and live among the brethren, and there you will find yourself only having authority over your rod." That is, having authority over the rod which he leans on. This will make him subdue himself to the troubles in the monastery, tolerating them and showing if he truly has a pure heart or not.

Discover your mistakes. Many monks discover the mistakes of their brethren but not their own. Talking about others sins makes them forget about their own sins. St. Moses the Black on the contrary would say, "these are my sins following me and here I am coming to judge my brother!" He was always thinking of his sins.

It happened one time that St. Pisarion was sitting with the brethren. They were judging a brother and dismissed him. St. Pisarion rose up and left saying, "as long as they are dismissing the sinners, I should go because I am a sinner like him."

The person who thinks about his sin lives a life of repentance. In monasticism we aim to examine ourselves, to know our weaknesses, and to practise abandoning them.

Monasticism and Humility:

Monasticism requires a life of humility. One of the virtues of monasticism is that the person should live in humility, feeling he is unworthy and everyone is better than himself. This is partial humility. He lives like the angels through this humility, not boasting over anyone, or blaming or getting upset, never asking for a position of leadership and does not grieve if he does not achieve it. Many monks lived a life of humility.

There are people who lived a life of humility without being monks. Anba Reweis who was a great saint lived as a monk without being consecrated or living in a monastery. He was a monk without clothes, without a title, a monastery or even a monastic name. His name was 'Reweis' which was the name of the camel he owned, but his original name was 'Freig' or 'Tigi'.

There are some people who lived as monks but they refused to be consecrated. Not only during the days of the early saints but of present times. Bishop Theophilus told us a story about a person named 'brother Awadallah' who lived in the monastery for 40 to 50 years without being consecrated as a monk. He always refused to be consecrated whenever they asked him. He lived as a righteous layman.

Monasticism is not the black attire which we wear, but it is the life. We may find that we sometimes say 'so and so is a true monk.' Are there monks who are not 'true monks?' Yes, there are some monks by name only, rather than living the true life of a monk. They live in the monastery but virtue does not live in their heart.

The true monk is a humble quiet person, dealing easily with all people. He accepts orders and rebuke easily. If another one is higher than himself in rank or ordination, he takes it easily and lets go of a hurtful word. If someone overlooked or forgot to greet him, he is not upset. There are some people who are very hard to deal with. They have harsh manners and are always troubling themselves and the monks around them.

Monasticism and Virtue:

Monasticism is a life of virtue. Let us ask ourselves: what is the virtue that I have gained during all these years as a monk? It is not a matter of who has been a monk for a longer time than another, but rather how many years have I been living in virtue which have been mastered? In which aspect was I so disciplined and placed the Lord in front of my eyes at all times?

St. Theophilus once met a monk who asked him, "Father, what did you master during all these years?" He answered, "believe me my father, there is nothing better for a person than to blame himself in everything." It is evident that this is a special virtue that he kept mastering for 40 years or so. As for you, what is the virtue which you have mastered so far?

After reading the book of 'The Ladder' written by St. John, a person once said to me, "I am not a monk yet. I could spend my entire life mastering one step. How could anyone finish all 30 steps!?" Ahead of you are the 30 steps of St. John Climacus, how many steps have you mastered? From dying to the world, estrangement, asceticism, repentance, tears, humility...many virtues. Which one of them did we master in monasticism? Monasticism is not just a matter of locking up ourselves for a few days in our cell.

Some may think that being virtuous in monasticism goes hand in hand to promotions of all ranks, from a monk to a priest, then a hegumen, then an Abbot and then a bishop. Another might think about administrative promotions, or supervising a certain place, then having a position in a Diocese...etc. These are all deviations from the correct target, created by their imagination and pleasing themselves.

When you left your home, your family, your job and your city, with your heart filled by the love of God and inspired by the lives of St. Anthony, St. Paul and many other saints whom you know...where did your fervent zeal go? What is your target? Do other targets occupy your heart? Did you forget your first target, for which you had left your home? Is it sufficient for you to wear the black robe and the hood, to be called a monk and father, while people ask you to absolve them?

What have you gained from monasticism? There are people who are more humble, sensitive, and closer to God in their prayers before becoming monks. What is the target of monasticism in your life? How far are you progressing? Is there any deviation from the target and if so to what extent?

Monasticism and Prayer:

Monasticism is a life of prayer, and prayers should be developing. After becoming a monk someone prays the Seven Agpia prayers, a matter which he did not do before monasticism. Then he goes to a higher level praying the Psalmody praises as well. He then adds the prayers of the prophets and saints. Still feeling that it is not enough, he starts practising prayers during work, while walking and sitting with people. Furthermore, he enjoys prayers at nights and vigils, remembering the verse, "Behold, bless the Lord, all you servants of the Lord, who by night stand in the house of the Lord! Lift up your hands in the sanctuary and bless the Lord." (Ps. 134:1). Also remembering St. Arsanius who used to start praying at sunset with the sun behind him, until it came in front of him! Prayers became for him as breathing.

Let us remind ourselves that with quantity there must also be quality. Where is the fiery prayer, with tears, understanding, humility, awe, faith, and love? Where is the prayer when a person feels the relationship between himself and God? Therefore it needs length and depth. This is one virtue in prayer, it needs growth and development. If such a one is asked by someone what he has achieved, he would answer, "I still have a long way to go and I am still a beginner."

A monk might desire the life of serenity since monasticism is a life of serenity. He then starts looking for the outer serenity of the senses, then the mind, the heart and feelings. He becomes like a seabed where nothing can disturb him, no matter how many troubles are around him. He becomes a very quiet person living the life of serenity. Someone might say how is it possible to practise serenity while people around are disturbing me? Father so and so did this and father so and so did that? Here we ask him, if you are judging others how can you live in serenity? His heart is disturbed from the inside, thus he sees everything before him as disturbed. If he calms himself from inside, everything around him will look calm.

A person who is calm would never be disturbed from anything. The life of serenity has quiet features, feelings and thoughts. Even his movement is quiet while another person makes noise while walking, waving his hands here and there speaking loudly.

I am afraid for you, lest monasticism is just titles. If someone would ask you 'what is monasticism?' You would answer 'as written in the books....'

Monasticism is the life of continuous prayer, serenity, quietness, repentance, purity of the heart and celibacy. Where are you regarding all these things?

Self-Account:

We have to sit for self-examination from time to time. When we talk about monasticism we have to follow one of the saints who said "what did we do which pleased God, and what did we do which upset God?"

Give a self-account every day considering it the last day of your life in order to reform yourself. Pray for your sins and be humble. Have pity over other people's weaknesses and focus on yourself instead of focusing on others. Thus, a person should count the virtues of monasticism and use them as a scale for his own life.

Be disciplined in your life. Stay away from anything which causes your destruction. A monk should have spiritual awareness. For a layman spiritual awareness is to notice his sins, but for a monk it is to notice his sins and to look for the spiritual virtues. To find out which virtues he has and which are missing in his life. He struggles with fasting, praying to the Lord to support his weakness, and feeling in need for special grace from God to progress.

It is very important to remember our monasticism and our life style because we will give an account to God for the spiritual capabilities which were given to us. Some people would wish to spend one night in the monastery, and would thank God fervently if they get that chance, while another one would consider himself unworthy of this grace of spending a week in the monastery. What about you who live in the monastery? How are you using the life of solitude with the places of the saints? What have you done with the talent of living in the house of the Lord all the days of your life? "One thing I have desired of the Lord, that will I seek: That I may dwell in the house of the Lord all the days of my life." (Ps 27:4). Remembering this fact, David says, "Blessed are those who dwell in Your house; They will still be praising You." (Ps 84:4). Do you bless Him forever while living in His house? "Behold, bless the Lord, all you servants of the Lord, who by night stand in the house of the Lord!" (Ps 134:1). This Psalm befits you because you are a servant of the Lord standing in the house of the Lord.

Living in the house of the Lord is a privlege which you will give an account for. Have you used it appropriately? Many people are jealous because you are living in the house of the Lord, right next to the church. The church is your house, next door to your cell! People are envious because you attend daily Liturgy and the Midnight Prayers. There are some people who would love to pray, but they may be watched by others and be ridiculed. You, the monk, do not have these obstacles!

People are jealous because each one of you has his private room. No one can enter and you can close your door and spend special time with your Father in Heaven. You live in a quiet calm atmosphere, while people dwelling in cities are surrounded with so much noise.

There are people who would love to live your lifestyle: in the house of God, in serenity, in separate cells, in the church with daily Liturgies and Midnight prayers. It is a spiritual atmosphere. You are living in harmony with one group of people who have one aim, which is the love of God and spending special time with Him. What have you done with this privlege?

It is not only laymen who are jealous, even our fathers the bishops would love to live in the same atmosphere as you. You might hear someone saying, "If I am given just one month to live in the monastery I would become a saint." God has given you months and years, what have you done with this privledge?

These are gifts offered to us from God to use them. Let us thank the Lord for giving us bountifully, and ask Him for grace to use them appropriately.

If an alert monk loses one day without doing any spiritual deed, he would make up for it the next day.

But a reluctant monk would spend days and months doing nothing without noticing it. All days are the same for him, and so, he would easily go back to his life as he was in the world, not benefiting anything from monasticism. If someone would go and visit his relative who had been a monk for a year or so, expecting him to be an earthly angel or a heavenly being he would be in shock to find him still the same, nothing changed from when he was a layman.

What have you done to become one of the earthly angels? Which rite have you practiced from among the rites of the angels, since monasticism is a rite of the angels? Nothing. Let us wake up, be aware of our monasticism, and use the gift granted to us. If we are too busy with work at the monastery and cannot live the life of continuous prayers, let us live the life of continuous love, or continuous tolerance.

Forgive Your Brother - Judge Yourself:

Practise forgiving others. Practise to relate other people's sins to you. Practise giving a sweet word and dealing calmly. Practise serving and obeying all. You can do many good things. One of the reasons for murmuring is thinking of the things which we do not have instead of offering thanks for what we have.

I wish that each one of us would try to progress, to stop defending ourselves, to discover our weaknesses, to stop depending on our intelligence, our experience, and our gifts. To stop seeking the monastery's recognition of the great works we are doing.

Sitting with my confession father should be a session of condemning myself, not for justification. If many monks have the same confession father, the father during the confession might not hear the monks confessing their sins during the confession, yet he would know who annoyed each other, and who fought with each other. Still, the confession father cannot reveal other brethren's confessions. All he can do is encourage the monk to confess any forgotten sins, but the monk would insist that there is none!

What would the confession father do when he knows that he is sitting with a monk who is either lying, or pitying himself, or his spiritual values are shaken, not knowing right from wrong? Such monks need to go back to the original monastic principles as seen in the saints of early monasticism and their teachings. These include St. Anthony the Great, St. Isaiah the Recluse, St Personofius, St. John of Assiut, and St. Felixinos. The words of these saints are correct principles, like a spiritual mirror through which we can discover ourselves when we look at it. This is what we need to measure ourselves according to the scale of the early fathers' sayings.

We should not only think about our sins, but also about our development. Are we progressing or are we stuck on one level? Sometimes we may be even going backwards. Are you growing in monastic virtue, in prayer, in living calmly, in loving God, in humility? Do you really feel it taking place when you rise up your hands in the morning and pray "When the morning hour approaches, O Christ our God the true light, let the senses and the thoughts of light shine upon us"? Do you feel that there is love between you and God? Do you feel that you have established a personal relationship with God in your monasticism? Do you feel that God is in your heart and you are in His heart? Are you experiencing the love for which people lived in the wilderness and caves for years, and they never became bored because they enjoyed God who is dwelling inside them? What has happened to you?

Let us test ourselves as St. Isaac says, "If you lose the way, sit with yourself. Remind Mary of her adultery and Israel of its defeat." Remind and rebuke yourself because of your many sins. St. Makarious the Great said, "Judge yourself, my brethren, before they judge you." St. Anthony the Great said, "If we judge ourselves, God will be pleased" and "If we remember our sins, God will forget them but if we forget them, God will remember them." Let us always remember this.

There are plenty of books and sermons about monasticism. We all have access to them and can learn. Each one should be alert and look out for his own salvation - that should be our only aim. If we are going in a different way from our salvation, we should change and correct our path, lest we should find many laymen entering before us to the heavens. While we are unaware, there may be many laymen who love and fear God more than us, being more humble. We may even consider ourselves as fathers who have authority over them, while they consider themselves the least, yet look at their high spiritual level!

It is written: "exhort one another daily" (Heb.3: 13). Let us remind each other continuously about these issues. In our spiritual struggle, we have to ask God always to grant us the power to reach our aim.

At all times, pour yourself before God saying, 'O Lord, who led St. Anthony in the mountain when he was alone, without anyone or a spiritual father to explain anything for him. You announced Your wisdom to him; give me also this free gift from You. O Lord, who led St. Paul the Hermit without anyone supporting him, support me as well. O Lord, who accepted the repentance of Pelagia, Mary the Egyptian and Moses the Black, guide me as You have guided them.'

Cling to God at all times saying, "I will not let You go until You bless me." Do not boast if you find yourself living in the right path, having corrected your mistakes and grown in grace. Remember the high levels which the saints have reached and compare yourself to them. Have I reached the level of St. Makarious of Alexandria, in his continuous prayer? Did I reach the depth or the sweetness of the lives of the saints? I still have a long road to go.

May God who granted the saints to enjoy Him and bless His Holy Name, grant us this privlege also.

THE READINGS DURING THE CONSECRATION OF A MONK

At the beginning of the consecration of a monk, there are verses read to him from the Old Testament. There is a particular reading about our father Abraham and his sojourn, "Get out of your country, from your family and from your father's house, to a land that I will show you. I will make you a great nation; I will bless you and make your name great; and you shall be a blessing. I will bless those who bless you, and I will curse him who curses you; and in you all the families of the earth shall be blessed." (Gen.12: 1). Also from Deuteronomy 8:3, "man shall not live by bread alone; but man lives by every word that proceeds from the mouth of the Lord." And from Joshua the son of Sirach we read, "My son, when you come to serve the Lord, prepare yourself for trials."

Let us now contemplate on the verses said to the

monk on the day of his consecration, to know the aim of these readings lest we should forget our monasticism or the things said to us on that day.

Genesis Chapter 12: The life of sojourn

Abraham was told to leave his country, family, and father's house for the sake of God. He was told to leave his previous life in order to start a new life with God. It is the same for the monk; he moves to a new family and becomes a son of the monastery.

Why did God tell Abraham to leave his country, family and father's house? Abraham was told this so that he could worship the Lord in the wilderness. We remember that Abraham always had the tent and the altar. The tent is a symbol of the life of sojourn and the altar the life of worship. He who lives in a tent does not have a permanent residence, like the hermits. That is why someone wrote a book about our father Abraham titled "Abraham the Hermit". He used to move from one place to another, rather than settling in one place.

God said to Abraham "Get out of your country, from your family and from your father's house, to a land that I will show you", there "I will make you a great nation; I will bless you and make your name great; and you shall be a blessing. I will bless those who bless you, and I will curse him who curses you." Thus it is a sojourn connected to blessing. We keep sojourning if we want God's blessing as He will bless us and make us a blessing. Abraham was a blessing to the entire world because his descendants formed the people whom the Lord had chosen in the Old Testament to bear His Name. He was also a blessing to Lot who was captured.

It is very nice to remember on the day of consecrating a monk that he himself becomes a blessing, "I will bless you, and you shall be a blessing." Sometimes people ask: what are the monks doing for the sake of the world? They do not work or toil! There are laymen who exert more effort in preaching than monks! The answer is that it is enough that these monks are a blessing to the world. We find a reference to this in the story of our father Abraham when he interceded for Sodom, "Let not the Lord be angry, and I will speak but once more: Suppose ten should be found there?" And He said, "I will not destroy it for the sake of ten." (Gen.18:23). This highlights that just the presence of those ten righteous people were a blessing to the city. Their presence alone would be a blessing that could save the city from destruction.

God was going to destroy the whole nation of the children of Israel. He said to Moses, 'Let me destroy this nation and I will make of you a great nation' but He did not do so for the sake of just one person, Moses. There are some people who are a blessing to the entire world.

In the early 1950's when we published the Sunday School Magazine I titled one of its cover pages, 'The Blessing of Noah' – the entire world was going to be destroyed by the flood, but a few human beings survived due to the blessing of Noah. We are all children of Adam and Noah. Noah and his children restored the world's population, and they received the blessing which was once given to Adam. Thus monks are a blessing to the world. Ask yourself: Am I truly a blessing? You may humble yourself but how does society judge you? How do others judge you? Do they actually see you as a blessing to the world?

After praying the introductory prayers "Our Father" and the "Thanksgiving Prayer" during the consecration, the part related to Abraham is prayed to remind us that it is a life of sojourn from both your side and God's side. He will make you a blessing. Sometimes you just see someone and say to yourself 'this person is a blessing!' Such was the case with Elijah in the house of the widow. He was a blessing and God blessed her entire house because of him. Joseph the Righteous was a blessing in the land of Egypt and in his own house. When we read about the Shunammite woman making an upper room on the roof of her house to host Elisha, we might wonder why did she do this? She felt he was a man of God and his presence would be a blessing in her house.

I remember a story which I heard from bishop Mina El Samueli, the first abbot of the monastery. He was one of the known fathers who went to the one of the surrounding villages late at night. Once he could not find a house to spend the night in and he went to the cashier of the village, who was a Christian, to spend the night yet the cashier did not allow him to sleep in his house. It then happened that a non-Christian woman saw him and she felt that he was a man of blessing, so she invited him to her house to spend the night. When he asked her if she needed anything from God, she answered that she did not have any children. He told her that she would have a child. She asked him, "what should I name him?" He said, "Hasan the one-eyed." After a while it happened that she actually had a son and she called him 'Hasan'. Later on he had an accident and lost one of his eyes, and the people used to call him "Hasan the one-eyed."

Another group of people that are a blessing are the spiritual fathers of the church. For example, when a father is visiting an area each family will race to host him as his presence is a blessing. Even his possessions can be a blessing, such as the cup of the late bishop

Abraam of Fayoum in which he used to drink, and the cross which bishop Sarabamoun the Veiled used to carry. Therefore the person and his possessions are a blessing.

Are you a blessing in your life? Does everything you touch become a blessing? How can you be a blessing? You can be blessing when you; live a life of sojourn like Abraham, leave everything for the sake of the Lord, live the life of worship like that of Abraham living in Canaan not returning to Ur or Haran. Thus the first part of the reading is "Get out of your country, from your family and from your father's house" and the last verse is, "he built an altar to the Lord."

Deuteronomy Chapter 8: God cares for His people in the wilderness

This reading is a continuation of the part read previously about Abraham's sojourn leaving his country and family for the sake of God. The reading demonstrates God's care for His people in the wilderness: "Every commandment which I command you today you must be careful to observe, that you may live and multiply, and go in and possess the land of which the Lord swore to your fathers. And you shall remember that the Lord your God led you all the way these forty years in the wilderness, to humble you and test you, to know what was in your heart, whether you would keep His commandments or not." (Deu 8:1)

This means that God has allowed you to live with Him in the wilderness, testing you whether you would keep His commandments or not. There may be someone who is living in the wilderness but not reflecting works fit for an ascetic. He may wear the clothes of a monk but not act like a monk. He makes promises to the Lord but is not committed to them. Thus it is written, "The Lord your God led you in the wilderness to know whether you would keep His commandments or not." (Deu 8:2).

This reading shows that the Lord humbled you, allowed you to hunger, and fed you with manna that He might make you know that man shall not live by bread alone, but by every word that proceeds from the mouth of God. Your garments did not wear out on you, nor did your foot swell these forty years. You should know in your heart that as a man chastens his son, so the Lord your God chastens you. "Therefore you shall keep the commandments of the Lord your God, to walk in His ways and to fear Him. For the Lord your God is bringing you into a good land, a land of brooks of water, of fountains and springs, that flow out of valleys and hills; land of wheat and barley, of vines and fig trees and pomegranates, a land of olive oil and honey; a land in which you will eat bread without scarcity, in which you will lack nothing." (Deu 8:6-9). Therefore from this we see how much God is caring for us.

Ask yourself, do you feel that the Lord is caring for you in the wilderness? Or rather are you looking out only for yourself, wanting to obtain your rights in every matter, controlling your circumstances rather than being dependant on the life of faith? This behaviour is not appropriate with God. With God we are walking in the wilderness and He is providing the manna. The cloud is a shadow for us and the pillar of fire is guiding us. He provides manna and water from a rock. We live in the wilderness by every word that proceeds from the mouth of the Lord. Notice that our Lord Jesus referred to this verse during the temptation on the mountain.

This chapter also shows us the spiritual food which the monk needs. I wish that each monk, while these words are being read, would ask himself, "Am I living by every word that proceeds from the mouth of the Lord? What is my relationship with the words of the Lord since my consecration? If God humiliated or made me suffer from hunger, would I rebel like the children of Israel? Would I be without worry and say that God is my supporter? God wants to test us in the wilderness to know what is inside our hearts, whether we are keeping His commandments or not?

God wants to know what is inside your heart rather than your outer appearance. You should know that as a man chastens his son, so the Lord your God chastens you. He will bring you into a good land, a land of brooks of water, fountains and springs. This good land is the spiritual life. If you are living a correct spiritual life you will feel that God is bringing you to a land of brooks of water, fountains and springs. You will flourish everywhere and live in the mountains.

Water is a symbol of the Holy Spirit, "...out of his heart will flow rivers of living water. But this He spoke concerning the Spirit, whom those believing in Him would receive." (John 7: 38-39). You will eat your bread abundantly if you live a proper monastic life, because you will live a life where there is no scarcity in the Lord. You will live a joyful life eating directly from the Tree of Life. You may say that there is a Cherubim holding the sword of fire infront of the tree of life, but God is saying to him 'Put your sword back in its sheath, for the path to the tree of life is now opened.' "To him who overcomes I will give to eat from the tree of life." (Revelation 2:7). God is feeding you the spiritual food and you need nothing else, "whoever drinks of the water that I shall give him will never thirst. But the water that I shall give him will become in him a fountain of water springing up into everlasting life." (John 4: 14). He will bring you into "a land of wheat and barley, of vines and fig trees and pomegranates, a land of olive oil and honey." (Deu 8:8). Wheat and vines are the blessing which Jacob took from his father Isaac, "with grain and wine I have sustained him." (Gen.27: 37), and grain and wine symbolise priesthood in the New Testament. Although Jacob did not experience priesthood, it was the blessing which came from his seed which blessed the entire earth, "in your seed all the families of the earth shall be blessed." (Acts 3: 25). On Maundy Thursday, the grain and wine are mentioned as bread and wine, symbolic of priesthood.

The work of the Holy Spirit can be symbolised to an olive. The olive tree is a symbol of the church living by the Holy Spirit. It is written in the book of Zechariah that there are two olive trees: the olive tree of the New Testament and the olive tree of the Old Testament. Our teacher St. Paul the Apostle says, "being a wild olive tree, were grafted in among them." (Romans 11:17), "Your children like olive plants all around your table." (Ps. 128:3). The olive symbolises the Holy Spirit and peace. Therefore you are under the care of God, both when you experience blessings or tribulations.

Joshua son of Sirach: "My son, when you come to serve the Lord, prepare yourself for trials."

This reading tells a monk to prepare his heart for trials, and to be strong and patient in them. Believe me, if a monk does not face trials, then there is something wrong with his monasticism. The devils envy every beautiful spirit; it troubles the kingdom of the devil. If you are not facing temptations maybe it is because you are not walking in the right path with the Lord. Ask yourself: is it possible that the devil is leaving me for a period? Does he feel that you are not affecting his authority or kingdom? I hope that whoever hears this verse would meditate on the kinds of temptations faced by the saints in the life of monasticism, and what blessings and benefits they gained.

I remember a wonderful sentence said by St. Anthony to his disciple St. Paul the Simple. St. Paul the Simple lived under St. Anthony's care and prayers for a few years. It happened once that St. Anthony said to him, "That is enough. I will arrange a far cave in the mountain for you to live in." St. Paul then answered, "My honourable teacher and dear father, I am happy living with you here." St. Anthony said to him, "No, you have to live alone and be exposed to the temptations of the devils." Observe the wisdom taught by St. Anthony! He showed St. Paul the importance of relying on God rather than to rely on another human being.

When St. Paul left St. Anthony and lived alone he faced the temptations of the devils. The result was that he started to perform miracles to the extent that sometimes even St. Anthony depended on him. For example, certain things that were not revealed to St Anthony were revealed to St. Paul. This is because he had faced the temptations of the devils. As it is written in the Paradise of the Holy Fathers, 'No one will be crowned except he who is victorious, and no one is victorious except he who fights.' Thus you have to be engaged in fights in order to be victorious.

It is a fact that we will face temptations. Let us not feel weak but rather let us endure and have patience. The temptation will not announce itself to you saying 'I am a temptation.' You may come across a day to day event that is disguised as a temptation. If you are warned about a temptation, then this may prepare you to be equipped to fight the temptation. However, if it comes disguised as a day to day event, such as your everyday dealing with others, then this temptation may reveal your inner self.

There are temptations to judge someone when you notice the mistakes of others in the monastery. But what do these negative thoughts achieve? You may even think to yourself, "what kind of monks are these and what kind of monasticism is this? My beloved, focus on yourself. You are just starting; you have to learn humility and meekness. You may think, 'shall I be humble to such people?' Are you only going to being humble to the saints? This mindset may cause harm and you may not be able to handle the temptation. A temptation may also come to someone in the monastery as a result of too much work. Another person could experience temptation of the thoughts. Each person experiences different kinds of temptation, but we say that you have to be strong and patient in them.

In your monasticism you have to ask yourself: are you being patient and strong in your trials? Do you gain benefit when others deal with you harshly? Do you tell yourself when you meet someone, 'he is carrying a blessing for me, let me take it?' Or is your life all about complaints, failures and judgements?

Frankly, I am telling you that those who prayed the prayers during the consecration are not in any way deceiving you. They did not stop only on the prosperous verse, "land of wheat and barley, of vines and fig trees and pomegranates, a land of olive oil and honey; a land in which you will eat bread without scarcity, in which you will lack nothing." (Deu 8:8). But lest you should think that it is all about enjoyment and pleasures, they also prayed, "My son, when you come to serve the Lord, prepare yourself for trials." (Sirach 2:1). Temptations will come; they may come from yourself, your colleagues at the monastery or from the devil.

It happened once that one of the monks became sick of the monastery that he thought to adopt the solitary life. Then it was said to him, "If you cannot bear the troubles coming from your brethren in the monastery, how would you tolerate the temptations coming from the devils in solitude?" The person, who can live successfully in the communal life of the monastery, can then live a successful life in solitude. The monk who lives in solitude is very strong and is not easily affected by trials.

"Accept whatever happens to you in periods of tribulations and be patient. For as gold is tested by fire, so are the chosen tested by tribulations." You should have humility and patience if you want to endure the fights and temptations in monasticism, otherwise you will not be successful in your monastic life. Even if the problem lasts for months or years, do not give up. Tell yourself 'I will never be shaken and my faith will not be weakened.' Say 'one day that person who is harsh to me will change his manners. God has sent these harsh words to me so that I may learn tolerance, forgiveness and love to those who trespass against me, and to know how to serve them.' Once a monk asked the abbot of the monastery to allow him to transfer to another monastery. When the abbot asked him if anyone had annoyed him, he answered, "Never, and that is the reason I want to go to another monastery. All the brethren here are saints. I could not find someone working against me to gain the virtue of loving my enemies. How could I gain those virtues while everybody is dealing in a saintly manner?" Therefore the Abbot knew that he was a serious monk and agreed to his request.

Evagrius said about continuous prayers, "Whoever starts continuous prayers should be patient with whatever trials he will face." So as long as you have started on the path of continuous prayers, do not grumble because the devils will not let you pray easily. This is why our fathers the saints wrote a lot about spiritual fights. Many saints wrote about the eight deadly sins fighting the human soul. Some of them are mentioned in the books of John Cassian, Evagrius and many others. The spiritual fights are temptations attacking you, yet no matter what temptations you might face, this is nothing compared to someone like St. Anthony. The devils used to physically appear and hit him. Once after being hit by the devil he said, "The hits were so strong that no human being could produce this strength."

The devils can attack in the form of tricks and deceiving visions. They can change themselves into the form of illuminating angels. It is possible to learn about false visions from the biographies of saints and from the lives of monks. These false visions and dreams have led many to destruction. Thus a monk needs two important things to combat the attacks of visions and dreams of the devil, which are discernment and guidance. A person who has discernment can differentiate spirits, as mentioned "test the spirits." (1 John 4: 1). Many who have gone astray did not consult others as it is written, "Those who are without a guide fall like tree leaves."

Humility of the spirit and long-suffering are tools we can use to fight the devils. St. Makarious the Great used to say that, "humility and poverty will make even the beasts submit to us." Once the devil appeared to St. Makarious and said, "We do exactly the same as you: you fast, but we do not eat at all, you stay awake and we never sleep, you live in the wilderness and we do also, but you overcome us with only one thing", St. Makarious asked him, "What is it?" To which the devil answered, "humility." Also St. Anthony says, "I saw the devil's traps spread over the entire world, so I knelt before God asking: 'Who could escape them?' and the Heavenly Voice answered, 'The humble person will escape them.'" Most of those who have fallen have had a degree of haughtiness of spirit. A humble person will conquer in monastic fights, even if the devil fights him face to face.

In the biography of the saints it is written that once the devil appeared to a monk in the form of an angel saying, "I am Archangel Gabriel. God has sent me to you." So the monk looked at him and said, "Maybe you are mistaken and should have been sent to someone else, because I am a sinner and do not deserve to see angels." The devil could not tolerate his humility and left him immediately. Ask yourself, do you have this humility which overcomes the devils?

By humility you can obtain victory throughout your monastic life. Monasticism does not need earthly power; it needs humility and long suffering. Those who think they are smart and can succeed in a spiritual life by themselves are deceived. By practising humility and long suffering, you will truly live successfully in your monastic life.

GOD'S PROMISES TO THE MONK

I wish every monk would remember the state in which he entered the monastery, the vows he made on the day of his consecration as well as God's promises. It is important that a monk reminds himself of these things from time to time.

God said, "This Book of the Law shall not depart from your mouth, but you shall meditate in it day and night, that you may observe to do according to all that is written in it." (Joshua 1:8). In the book of Deuteronomy, we see that God reminded His people about the law a second time so that they wouldn't forget it.

David the prophet says, "For Your law is my delight... I do not forget Your law... I do not forget Your commandments." (Ps 119:77).

God wants His people to remember certain events and miracles. For example, the manna that was kept in the Ark of the Covenant served as a constant reminder of God's care that He provided the Israelites with food in the wilderness. Aaron's rod was also kept so that they didn't forget about the time in which it blossomed. Twelve stones were set up as a memorial of when Joshua crossed the Jordan River. God wants us to remember certain events for our spiritual benefit.

We often go astray when we forget our vows and the goodness God has shown us. During the Liturgy, the priest reminds the congregation of the Lord's commandments when he says: "Every time you eat of this bread, and drink from this cup, you preach My death, confess My resurrection and remember Me till I come." How often do we receive the Holy Mysteries and forget about God?

God reminded the Israelites that they used to be strangers so that they can be hospital to foreigners. He told them: "you shall neither mistreat a stranger nor oppress him, for you were strangers in the land of Egypt." (Exodus 22:21)

The church helps us remember important events by consecrating fasts, celebrating feasts as well as special services and prayers. For example, the church remembers Christ's suffering every year during Passion Week, every day during the Sixth Hour prayer and through fasting every Friday. These are very beneficial because they help us remember the cross of Christ, His pains and great redemption. They remind us of His endless love and the fact that we were bought by His precious Blood. "For God so loved the world that He gave His Only Begotten Son." (John 3:16).

God made the Passover a feast so that people remember how He saved the Israelites from the angel of death. They wore their shoes, held their rods in their hands and ate in haste. Why? So that they can remember how God saved the Israelites and tell their children the story. Our life often becomes lukewarm because we forget many things.

A monk needs to remember the day of his consecration. How boldly he left his family, fled from marriage, pressures, wealth, prestigious positions, and in fact the entire world! We need to remember our original zeal. God does not want us to forget these things.

David the Prophet said, "Lord, make me to know my end, and what is the measure of my days, that I may know how frail I am." (Ps 39:4). In response to this request the church has organised daily prayers in the

Agpia to remind us of our departure from this world. In the litanies of the Twelfth Hour we pray, "Behold, I am about to stand before the Just Judge in fear because of my numerous sins" and "If this life was everlasting and this world eternal, O my soul, you would have a valid excuse." The gospel also reminds us of death as Simeon the Elder says, "Lord, now You are letting Your servant depart in peace." (Luke 2:29).

The church always reminds us of our departure from this world by referring to Judgement Day and the Bridegroom who will come at an hour we do not expect. God knows that we often forget. That is why He sends us many reminders.

The Holy Bible often warns us against pride and reminds us of our sins and weaknesses. "Remember therefore from where you have fallen, repent." (Rev 2:5). Who remembers the promises, vows and pledges that were made on your behalf on the day of your baptism? Who remembers how they renounced Satan and all his evil deeds? Do we actually remember these things?

The Sabbath is a day of rest. God wants to give us rest because weariness is a consequence of sin - it did not exist before Adam's fall. It was only when Adam sinned that God said, "Cursed is the ground for your sake, in toil you shall eat of it all the days of your life."

(Gen 20:8). This is why God gives us rest; rest is in Him.

God blessed the Sabbath day and made it a day for us to do His work. He didn't say, "Keep the Sabbath day holy" but "Remember the Sabbath day, to keep it holy." (Exodus 20:8). That is, God wants us to remember the Sabbath as a holy day.

We sometimes forget who we are. We wear monastic garments but monasticism is not in our hearts, on our mind or evident in our behaviour. We need to remember that we are monks and that on the day of our consecration the funeral prayers were prayed over us. If we have died to the world, how could we live like people in the world? Do you really believe that you died to the world, and that the world is but dust, wind and rubbish? "I count them as rubbish" (Phil 3:8). It is all vanity of vanities! He who believes that the things of the world are all vanity of vanities does not care about materialistic issues because the world means nothing to him. Monks receive a new name and wear new clothes as a symbol that the old person has died and that he is "transformed by the renewing of the mind" (Rom 12:2). Everything has changed, but are we really living this new life? Do we remember this transformation?

On the day of his consecration a monk needs to remember that he has died to the world and everything in it. He must not think about the world or bring it inside the monastery. He must not carry its desires or worries inside his heart. He is dead to the world.

When they brought St Arsanius his portion of inheritance, he said: "How could I inherit anything from a dead person when I died before him?" He also said: "I have always set the hour of my death before my eyes since I became a monk."

The problem is that we sometimes forget that we have died to the world. We need to remember that we were shrouded during the funeral prayers and had sad tunes sung over us. There are many sad tunes but let us remember "Agios". In this hymn we tell God, "You alone are Holy. You are the Almighty. We need to be holy like You but we can't because we are sinners. This is why we will always tell You that 'You alone are Holy.'"

The church sings "Agios" in every funeral prayer. We tell God that He is Holy and that the one who died is a poor person. We also ask Him to give us the "holiness without which no one will see the Lord." (Heb 12:14)

Remember monks are called "earthly angels" or "heavenly people". But are we really angels? Do people feel like a trip to the monastery is a trip to heaven? Do they say monks are angels? Why are we consecrated to be angels and don't live like angels? We have to remember that we were consecrated to become angels.

St. John Chrysostom said, "Heaven with its stars is not equal to the wilderness of Scetis with its angels". Let us be practical, is the wilderness of Scetis more pleased with its angels than heaven with its stars?

Believe me, it is not enough to self-reflect and assess our monasticism only once a year. We should be judging ourselves every day.

When St. Macarius saw the hermit fathers in the inner wilderness, he told his children: "I am not a monk, but I have seen monks." St. Anthony also had the same feeling when he saw St. Paul. If these are the feelings of St. Macarius and St. Anthony the Great, how should we feel? Are we proud or confident enough to say that we are pious and saintly monks and no one resembles us? How harsh is the rebuke of the spiritual elder who said, "until when, my brother, will you comfort yourself with these black garments?" Do you really think you are a monk just because you are wearing a black garment?

I hope we all remember the main monastic virtues. These are virtues we should all have. They are written in the books of the fathers and are known to everyone. If we did not know them, we would be excused; but we do know them. We often read "The Paradise of the Fathers" while we are eating. Some monks have already memorised the book, as well as many of the sayings of the fathers and the lives of the saints. We have no excuse. The more we know, the more will be asked of us.

One of the saintly fathers used to judge himself every day. He would ask himself: "Have you done anything that pleased God today? What have you done to upset Him?" Is monasticism living inside us and are we living it on a daily basis? Have we died to the world yet? Are we living a life of silence and continuous prayer?

Monks with responsibilities in the monastery, do you rebuke your brothers like one with authority? Did you forget that you are a monk? The spiritual elders tell us not to speak with authority to anyone. Those who complain about their cells and the food in the monastery, did you forget that you are a monk? The monks who meet visitors and start talking about worldly issues, did you forget that you have died to the world?

When will we remember that we are monks and live a true life of monasticism? Why do we read "The Paradise of the Fathers" while we are gathered on several occasions? We resolve every problem in a monastic manner because we are different to everyone else living in the world.

If a monk falls into any difficulty, he may start complaining and rebelling. His soul and mind become troubled. He forgets the words that were read on the day of his consecration, "My son, if you come to serve the Lord, prepare yourself for temptations." This is also read during the third hour of Tuesday during Passion Week.

We need to remember the monastic virtues, the lives of the saints and that we are called to live like earthly angels or heavenly people. The monastic life is a dream that has been desired by man before the fourth century.

People all over the world travel land and sea to hear a word of spiritual benefit from a monk. This is because monasticism is a school of practical wisdom for the spiritual life. People often ask monks: "Tell me a word for my salvation." A word for salvation? How beautiful is this understanding that spiritual words can save! This wisdom was named by some of the fathers such as St Isaac, who wrote much about this topic. Wisdom, knowledge and discernment in monasticism are not acquired from books but spiritual experiences.

Although knowledge is the aim of Sufism and asceticism, scholars of Sufism are called "those who know God". This was originally a Christian way of thinking as the Lord Jesus said in His famous long prayer, "And this is eternal life, that they may know You, the only true God." (John 17:3).

"Open my eyes that I may see wondrous things from Your Law." (Ps 119:18). Although Balaam was a man who perished, he made a wonderful statement that has been preserved, "The utterance of Balaam the son of Beor, the utterance of the man whose eyes are opened. The utterance of him who hears the words of God, who sees the vision of the Almighty." (Num 24:3-4). The Lord also said: "blessed are your eyes for they see" (Matt 13:16). Do you have this spiritual sight? What do you see?

What have you acquired from monasticism? Holiness? Knowledge? Experience? If you have not acquired these, when will you obtain them and how? Let every monk sit with himself and remember the beautiful life to which he has consecrated himself. The life which many of our fathers yearned for and preferred over the ranks of a patriarch or bishop, performing pastoral and priestly services. They fled to live this life which is full of mysteries.

A life of monasticism is full of wonderful mysteries. Those who tasted it were astonished. They could not tell if they were on earth, in spirit or in the body. A spiritual elder once said that a monk cannot express the moments he experiences because he is so stunned with the Lord!

These mysteries can only be explained through silence. The mind cannot comprehend them because they are above its level of understanding. No words can express them. Only the heart and spirit can feel them.

Monasticism is strange; it is full of mysteries. Those who lived a true life of monasticism lived the holy mysteries of God. I do not mean the seven mysteries (sacraments) of the church, but the mysteries of the spirit, spiritual knowledge and understanding; the mysteries of being present with God and the taste of Paradise.

Monks Are Earthly Angels

It is said that monks are "earthly angels". But what is an angel and why are monks likened to angels? Angels are spirits. "He makes His angels spirits, His ministers a flame of fire." (Ps 104:4). Therefore, if a monk is an angel, he is a person living with the spirit or living as a spirit. That is, he lives away from the body, away from material things and all its works.

To what extent should a monk be a spirit and live according to the spirit? How can one reject all the works of the body? By abstaining from the desires of the flesh, such as the desire for food. That is why monks are devout and fast much. They do not care about the desires of the flesh.

St. Macarius used to eat once a week during the Lent. When he visited the monastery of St Bakhomios, the monks observed this and were disturbed by his ascetism. They told St. Bakhomios that he had no body, for a body cannot live in such a manner.

Angels do not eat. The more a person controls his desire for food, the more his spirit grows. The body can overcome the spirit. Too much food leads to a troubled spirit; it weighs it down. Father Abdel Messih the Ethiopian used to walk in the wilderness like a deer – his body was light and his movements were gentle.

Monks are angels as they neglect their bodies' desire for food. We ought to read about the way our fathers the monks used to fast. When St Arsanius started to eat good food, he learnt a good lesson from Anba Isaiah. He then confessed: "I learnt Greek and Roman, but I did not comprehend the wisdom behind eating beans like that Egyptian."

In regards to abstaining from food or certain types of food that a person desires, we say: "Take away your hand while your soul still desires it". Do not allow yourselves to feast on what you desire, as one of our fathers said, "If you are given food that your soul desires, spoil its taste and then eat it." That is, change its taste by adding something to it, or mixing it with some salt before you eat it. Monks should not complain about food or ask for certain meals to be prepared – such are contrary to the nature of monasticism.

Monks should also subdue their bodies in purity and chastity. This is one of the vows of monasticism. More is expected from a monk in regards to chastity compared to laymen. This is because a monk should be modest in all aspects of his life – even in his clothes. He should not reveal any part of his body by any means.

St Isaac said: "a monk should preserve the chastity of his body and be modest even inside his cell." They should be modest in their dress, sleep, sitting position, in everything! If they are attacked by evil thoughts, they should not act upon them but rather resist them until death.

St Paul rebuked the Hebrews as they "have not yet resisted to bloodshed, striving against sin." (Heb 12:4). To bloodshed! He wanted them to avoid sin, even if it led to martyrdom.

A monk will be attacked greatly by impure thoughts, but he should never allow these thoughts to affect his bodily actions. Monks need to resist these thoughts as much as possible and distance themselves from anything that arouses such thoughts.

A monk is an angel in regards to food and chastity. He is an angel because he does not act upon his body's desire for food, sex, rest or sleep. As the Lord said, "The spirit indeed is willing, but the flesh is weak." (Mark 14:38).

The church encourages monks to be vigilant through the three services of the Midnight prayer. Those who do not attend the Midnight Praise are usually asleep – i.e. living according to the body. Of course this is not a monastic way of life, unless such a monk follows a special canon set by his confession father which requires him to stay up late or complete his duties like hermits.

Monks who spend the night in prayer resemble angels, but those who sleep lose the work of angels. Their body rules over them in food, chastity, rest and sleep. Monks resemble angels as they fight sleep and work to weary their bodies. The early fathers used to advise people to tire their bodies.

How do monks crucify the body with its desires? Monks tire their bodies when they deny themselves any rest, stand for prayer, serve their brothers or perform various services in the monastery. There are many examples of such monks found in the lives of the saints, such as Simon and Luke.

When the body becomes a slave to the spirit and will of a person, it does not ask for certain things. Angels are spirits. How can a monk be an earthly angel if he lives according to the desires of the flesh and gives his body rest? We need to examine ourselves and determine whether or not we are satisfying the desires of the flesh. We need to ask ourselves: am I fulfilling my body's desire for sleep or rest? How about my desire for food and concern for my appearance?

Some monks experience wars with their new appearance; they like to look handsome. This is war of the body.

St Paul of Tammuh severely wearied his body to the extent that the Lord appeared to him and said: "That's enough my beloved Paul". The saint replied saying: "My Lord, no matter how much I struggle, it is nothing compared to what You suffered for my sake."

Let us refer to "The Paradise of the Fathers" and the lives of the saints to learn how our fathers triumphed over the body and did not respond to its needs. Let us learn about how they struggled in vigilance, weariness, chastity and fasting.

Someone once asked St John the Short: "What is monasticism?" The saint answered, "It is tiresome for the sake of God."

Prostrations also tire the body. During fasting periods there are lots of prostrations. There are many other ways of crucifying the body but we cannot discuss them now. In the Catholic church they are called "mortifications". St Paul the Apostle said: "For Your sake we are killed all day long" (Rom 8:36) and "death is working in us." (2 Cor 4:12). Also during the ninth hour we pray, "Put to death our carnal lusts, O Christ our God, and deliver us". We pray this every day, but do we actually think about what it means? I will leave you to meditate upon this prayer and say that it means our senses should not engage in any activity that would tire the spirit. Our eyes should not look and our ears should not listen to things that would weary the spirit. Those who satisfy the desires of the flesh live according to the body, not according to the spirit.

A well-known virtue among monks is that of keeping one's senses from wandering. Monks can become disturbed by what they gather and hear about different subjects. The tongue can also tire a monk and disturb others. Eyes can also be a disturbance because of the scenes they see. Therefore, if a monk enters his brother's cell, he ought to not lift his eyes to see what is inside. That is, a monk should enter and leave his brother's cell without looking at its contents; otherwise he may be disturbed by his furniture, possessions or way of living.

Purity of Heart:

A pure heart leads to purity of the mind. A person who is suspicious and always doubting does not have a pure heart. A person with complicated thoughts is not pure. Monasticism is purity of the heart. If we start talking about the purity of the heart, we would be discussing total holiness. A person with a pure heart has pure senses and only speaks pure words, "For out of the abundance of the heart the mouth speaks." (Matt 12:34).

We need to always ask ourselves: "If there was an angel in my place what would he do? Would my guardian angel be ashamed of what I am doing?"

Psalm one says: "Blessed is the man who walks not in the counsel of the ungodly, nor stands in the path of sinners, nor sits in the seat of the scornful." We need to ask ourselves, "will my guardian angel feel ashamed to stand next to me?"

Another issue concerning angels is obedience. We often pray: "Thy will be done on earth as it is in heaven." That is, just as the angels carry God's will, we ought to do the same. How do the angels carry out God's will? They carry out His orders immediately, without arguing or discussing anything.

The Psalmist says, "Bless the Lord, you His angels, who excel in strength, who do His word, heeding the voice of His word." (Ps 103:20). This is because angels obey God's orders without arguing. God ordered the angel to strike all the first born and he obeyed without arguing or questioning. An angel's job is to carry out God's orders and not to discuss them. If you start thinking or arguing about anything you have been ordered to do, asking whether it is right or wrong, then you are not an angel. You may be a leader or one of the elders, but not an angel because angels always obey without any discussion.

A monk may be given an order but decide to postpone it to the next day. This is not obedience. An obedient monk immediately obeys. Angels do not postpone following orders.

Angels also refrain from materialistic possessions. This topic needs its own special talk in which we would discuss possessions and the love of material things. Yet, I remember that it was said about a monk that he gave up the whole world, with all its riches, and yet fought with his brothers about a needle. Has such a monk died to the world? Is he an angel?

Let us meditate on these things in our lives.

THE WORK OF GOD IN THE LIFE OF A MONK

We need to be vigilant for the salvation of our souls. However vigilance alone is not enough. God has to enter our lives and work with us; otherwise our toil and strife will be useless. Our spiritual lives are not merely dependent on our will but also on the work of God in our lives and the communion with the Holy Spirit, as the Lord says, "for without Me you can do nothing." (John 15:5).

Indeed, the salvation of the human race is the work of God. It was said about Christ that He shall be called "Jesus, for He will save His people from their sins." (Matt 1:21). Thus, the name "Jesus" means, "God is a Saviour" or "God saves". The names "Joshua" and "Isaiah" are derived from "Jesus".

Even in the Old Testament God wanted to remind the human race that salvation is obtained through Him.

In the book of Psalms, David often repeats "God my Saviour" and "the Lord is my strength and song, and He has become my salvation." (Ps 118:14).

In spiritual vigilance it is important to ask God to enter our lives and surrender to Him so that He may save us. God is the One who saves us. In our spiritual lives, we need to wait for the deliverance of the Lord. We need to stop and take a moment to meditate on His work.

God worked for six days and rested on the seventh day. However, this does not mean that He did not do any work on the seventh day. In fact, God saved the entire world on the seventh day. We are still living in the seventh day until the final resurrection. After all the Holy Bible did not mention that, "the evening and the morning were the seventh day".

God is the Almighty who controls the whole universe. How beautiful are the words of the Lord when He said, "My Father has been working until now, and I have been working." (John 5:17). God is always working.

He said: "I will not leave you orphans; I will come to you." (John 14:18). He is working with us. "For where two or three are gathered together in My name, I am there in the midst of them." (Matt 18:20). He is working in our midst.

He said that He has, "inscribed [us] on the palms of [His] hands" (Isaiah 49:16). He also said that "the very hairs of [our] head[s] are all numbered" (Matt 10:30) and that "not a hair will fall from [our] head[s]." (Acts 27:34). God is working.

"The Lord preserves the infants." (Ps 116:6). Here, the word "infants" refers to those living with the humility, innocence and simplicity of a child. It also refers to those who are unable to look after themselves, and hence submit their lives to God and other people. God protects those who are unable to protect themselves. They "shall abide under the shadow of the Almighty." (Ps 91:1).

I like the verse which says, "The Lord will fight for you, and you shall hold your peace." (Exodus 14:14). It implies that God is fighting our battle with all His strength and great power, while we hold our peace. It is difficult to hold our peace as every man wants to fight for himself and show off his skills, courage, strength, intelligence and excellence. However, those who hold their peace enjoy the salvation of the Lord and can say, "Not unto us, O Lord, not unto us, but to Your name give glory." (Ps 115:1). "The name of the Lord is a strong tower; the righteous run to it and are safe." (Prov 18:10).

I wish that we would all mediate on how God works in our life. Let us not think about our own work, but rather focus on the work of God. Remember the verse: "Unless the Lord builds the house, they labour in vain who build it; unless the Lord guards the city, the watchman stays awake in vain." (Ps 127:1).

Since our labour is in vain without the Lord, we need to ask ourselves: does God work in my life? Do I give Him the chance to build? Is He my guard or am I always fighting for myself, ensuring my rights using my own power? What is the work of God in my life?

How does God work in our life?

God can work in our lives directly or through His angels, saints and loved ones on earth. His own Divine intervention is evident when David said, "Yea, though I walk through the valley of the shadow of death, I will fear no evil; for You are with me" (Ps 23:4) and also in the case of the three saintly youth with the fourth who resembled the Son of God. Again David mentions God's Divine intervention when he says, "My rock is the Lord" (Ps 18:2).

However in Daniel's case, "God sent His angel and shut the lions' mouths." (Dan 6:22). Here, God sent His angel to save Daniel. Angels play important roles in the lives and salvation of many people. For example St Paul, St Peter and Elijah were all positively impacted by angels. God often sends saints and angels to do His work in our lives.

We should have a relationship with the saints and angels. Some people choose particular saints for certain requests or aspects of their lives. For example, a person who is tired of battling against evil thoughts may pray, "O Lord, send me St Moses the Black who struggled to resist these thoughts and went to his confession father eleven times in one night. Please St Moses the Black, help me fight these thoughts as you fought a similar war." Another person who may be fighting against the desires of the flesh may ask St Augustine or St Mary the Egyptian for help as they also fought this fierce battle. Those who may be suffering from theological thoughts may resort to St Athanasius, while those struggling in their monastic life may ask St Anthony. Similarly, those who need help in their strife to pray or keep vigil may resort to St Arsanious.

Do not stand alone in prayer. Build a relationship with God and His saints. Woe to the man who is alone, especially in his spiritual wars. I pity those who try to fight the devil on their own.

It is written, "And war broke out in heaven: Michael and his angels fought with the dragon; and the dragon and his angels fought." (Rev 12:7). We pray and say, "O Lord, the wars on earth are similar. Please send us Archangel Michael or one of Your other angels." We should not fight our spiritual battles alone or depend on our own struggles, will, power or vows. All of these are vain without God's support. We need to always ask God to enter our lives and work with us.

God can work in our lives even without us asking Him. However, we need to ask Him to work in our lives because He does not want to lead us against our will. St Augustine says, "God who created you without your will, does not want to save you without your will." Although God wants everyone to be saved, He does not impose His salvation on anyone. God wants us to do good deeds out of our own free will, not by force or out of obligation. If we ask God to enter our lives, He will work in powerful ways. If not, we need to pray and ask God to grant us this will and desire.

One cannot be happy if he lives alone but would find rest when he asks for God's presence and work in his life. The strongest man is the one who allows God to work in his life, regardless of how weak he is on his own. Conversely, the weakest man is the one who does not allow God to enter his life, regardless of how strong he is on his own. "[Sin] has cast down many wounded, and all who were slain by her were strong men." (Prov 7:26). That is, strong men who did not allow God to enter their lives were slain by sin. Therefore, we pray saying, "come Lord Jesus" (Rev 22:20) and enter our lives. "Let God arise, let all His enemies be scattered." (Ps 68:1). When we ask God to arise, we become like the disciples who woke up the Lord in the boat and said, "Teacher, do you not care that we are perishing?" (Mark 4:38). We need to ask God to arise; He wants us to ask Him.

God wants us to surrender our life and will to Him. He wants us to ask Him to enter our lives. Love is the most sensitive emotion. God does not want us to love Him by force. One may be forced to obey but he cannot be forced to love. God does not even want us to obey Him by force. He desires our hearts.

God says, "Come to Me, all you who labour and are heavy laden, and I will give you rest." (Matt 11:28). Here, He is not only referring to those who are heavy laden with life's responsibilities, problems, work and money, but also those who are weighed down by their sins or spiritual struggle. We need to tell God about our desires, spiritual struggles, temptations and the sins that weigh us down. Let us ask God to intervene and work in our lives because He loves to help us.

However, there is a level higher than just letting God work with us. St Paul says about himself and Apollo his colleague, "For we are God's fellow workers." (1 Cor 3:9). Notice how he did not say "God is working with us" but rather "we are working and God is working with us." God is the foundation, we work with Him. O Lord, we offer You our lives. You paid a great price for us; we are Yours. You always work in our lives. Allow us to work with You. You protect the church as it is Your House; we are just working with You.

Whenever we pray with David, "Create in me a clean heart", God works within us and purifies our heart. We are nothing; we cannot cleanse our own hearts. It is strange how so many people frequently pray this psalm but do not believe that God is the One who will purify their hearts. Do you understand the words you are praying in psalm 51 "Create in me a clean heart, O God and renew a steadfast spirit within me"? God is the One who renews. "Purge me with hyssop, and I shall be clean; wash me, and I shall be whiter than snow." God is the one who washes and purifies us. These words remind us that it is God who works inside us and purifies us. We are not the one who is working. I hope we all feel this way when we pray.

If you ever feel that your heart, words, conscience and life is pure, do not think that this is due to your own work or efforts. Do not be deceived and fall into self-righteousness. We need to remind ourselves that God is the one who cleanses us. We cannot acquire this purity on our own. By doing this, we will always remember the work of God inside us.

The Person Also Has A Role:

Continuously strive so that God may enter your life. Ask God to deliver you. Do not just apologise for the sins you have committed and say "Have mercy upon me, O Lord". Rather confess and say, "O Lord, I cannot overcome this sin. You can save me. I am weaker than the devils. Work with me. I want to see Your work. I know that You are able to save me; I want to see Your salvation."

I like the psalm that says: "Lord, You have been favourable to Your land" and "show us Your mercy Lord, and grant us Your salvation" (Ps 85:1,7). That is, Your mercy is present but I want You to show it to me. I am like Thomas - I want to touch it with my hands and see. Give me a chance to see this mercy, talk about it and rejoice that it may comfort me in all my future tribulations.

Our Lord does good works all the time. I wish that we could see God performing such good works. He is the Almighty who can see everything. He knows our tribulations to deliver us. He notices our sins to save and purify us. He can also see our fights and struggles. He keeps a record of everything. We ought to confess our weaknesses and pray about them, so that God may work within us.

Tell Him, "Lord, please work for the sake of Your church and congregation. Work for the sake of my soul which is Your temple and house. Your house should be holy for You said, "My house will be called a house of prayer". As long as my soul is Your house, I ask You to turn it into a house of prayer. If that requires You to make a whip of cords to purify the temple of my soul to dismiss the sellers and overturn the tables of the money-changers, please do so. Work for that sake of Your glory and allow me to see it."

We need to believe in the work of God in our lives. The devil may try to lead us into despair and make us feel as though God is not working within us or has abandoned us. He might also make us feel as though our sins have separated us from God that He does not hear our prayers and that everything we do is in vain. But the truth is that God works in our lives and that He comes to save us, even in the fourth watch of the night or at the eleventh hour. He comes and uses us even at the last moment of our lives, like He did with the right hand thief. It may appear that God is delayed but this maybe so that we have a chance to deepen our prayer, fasting, faith and patiently wait for the Lord. Remember the verse, "Wait on the Lord; be of good courage, and He shall strengthen your heart." (Ps 27:14).

If we are struggling to fight a specific sin for a long time, we should not be disturbed but rather, "wait on the Lord; be of good courage, and He shall strengthen [our] heart[s]." Notice that the verse does not say that we will be strong and of good courage when the Lord delivers us, but rather "be of good courage, and He shall strengthen you heart." That is, we need to be strong in faith and courageous before the Lord delivers us.

I feel that the Lord will definitely come. In psalm 70, our father and teacher David wrote: "Make haste, O Lord, to deliver me… You are my help and my deliverer, O Lord, do not delay". Believe me, I often read those words and wonder if God really does hasten or delay. God's timing is fixed. He never hastens or delays. His timing is perfect, to the minute and second. Do not think that God is delayed in helping you. Do not ask God to hasten because He always comes at the most appropriate time, even if it is the fourth watch, the eleventh hour or the twenty-fourth hour. In His wisdom, He chooses the most appropriate time to work such that it may be precise and beneficial. It is not up to us to tell God to hasten or delay. No, He comes to us without our prayers or request.

The paralytic at the Pool of Bethesda had no one to carry him into the water for 38 years. The Bible mentions that "Jesus found him" (John 5:14) and healed him. The paralytic did not ask Jesus to heal him. Similarly, God often comes to us without our request. He gently touches and works with us. We need to see the way God works in the life of people without their request. There are many situations like this recorded in the Holy Bible. For example, when Miriam and Aaron humiliated Moses, God interfered without Moses asking. God also interfered when Jonah was in the belly of the fish and when the three saintly youth were in the fiery furnace. The youth did not ask the Lord to stop them from being burnt, but were rejoicing that they could be considered martyrs.

God works in marvellous ways. We should never think that God abandons us in our tribulations or when we sin. There is a beautiful verse that says, "in all their affliction He was afflicted, And the Angel of His presence saved them" (Is 63:9). It is as if God is afflicted when we are afflicted. It is difficult to say that God is afflicted, but that is what the verse says. "Rejoice with those who rejoice, and weep with those who weep." (Rom 12:15). Similarly, God cries when we cry and rejoices when we rejoice. He shares all our feelings. Let us also invite God to share all our deeds, whether big or small. If we train our senses and have sensitive faith, we would feel the hand of God in all our deeds. We would feel it and rejoice.

Twenty years ago, I thought about writing a book titled, "God's Hands in Incidents" about the way God works in the lives of people, in every single incident of their lives. God works but we just do not see. If we did, we would see God working in ways which surpass our understanding, even during those times when we think He is sleeping in the ship.

It is good to keep vigil, but we need God to work with us.

Monastic Life Is Different To Worldly Life

Monasticism And Talking:

People may talk much in the world, but a monk's words should be limited. There is an illness called the 'disease of talking'. We need to know the causes of this disease, its problems and how to treat it.

Excessive talking is inappropriate in monasticism, particularly destructive talk. Destructive talk can plant doubt and introduce thoughts in our minds that can be hard to get rid of. It can also encourage complaints, create problems and opposition, thus keeping people in a troubled state.

Talking is inappropriate for monasticism as it is a waste of time. Monks should rather spend such time on things that would build themselves up; but to waste time in talking is a disease.

In the world, people talk much. If one chooses to remain silent he is often asked for the reason why he is not talking. People may even think that he is upset or grieving. However in monasticism if one is talking without benefitting others he is destroying himself and wasting his time.

Some monks reach a high level of spirituality within a short period of time. For example, St Maximous and St Domadious. Despite being quite young, their prayers were like tongues of fire ascending to heaven. Also, St Misael became a hermit at the age of seventeen. Do you think he had time for talking?

Those who take their spiritual lives seriously are busy with their salvation. They live a life of continuous prayer, and hence do not have time to waste talking to others.

St Mina was martyred at the age of 23. When did he become a monk? When was he granted the gift of healing? How did he fill the world with miracles? The answer lies in the fact that he was serious about his spiritual life; he was always working. He had no time to waste talking to others.

Once St Macarius the Alexandrian asked St Arsansius: "My father, why do you avoid sitting with us?" The saint answered: "God knows that I love you all, but I cannot talk to both God and man." Such is the man who earnestly seeks his salvation. Yet others continuously destroy both themselves and their acquaintances as they fill each other with vain thoughts and talk. What is the reason behind all this destruction? It is the disease called 'talking'.

The fathers say that those who talk much are empty inside. The tongue speaks if it is not busy with God, when there is no prayer, meditation or self-reproach. People talk when they are not busy doing something beneficial, when they do not understand the value of their time. Talking is a disease which destroys the spiritual work of a man, stops his prayers, immobilises his relationship with God and even halts his thought development.

Those who understand the value of their time focus on building up themselves spiritually. They spend much of their time reading the sayings of the fathers, the lives of the saints, the Holy Bible and memorising its verses. They become a treasure of knowledge because of their readings.

It was said about Origen that he used to hire

bookshops so that he can spend the whole night reading. Also, St. Athanasius published two great books when he was about twenty years of age – "A Message to the Atheists" and "On The Incarnation". He was so full of knowledge that he spoke at the Council of Nicea when he was just a youthful deacon. From a young age he understood that his time was valuable, and hence made the most of every minute.

Some people choose to sit and speak for hours. During this time they could have read a whole book! Being filled with the words and knowledge of God is better than talking. Those who talk are emptying themselves without being filled.

Some people like to complain to others about their problems whenever they feel overwhelmed. However, the person in which they are confiding to is often innocent and has nothing to do with their problems. If you were to ask both of them about what they have gained, they would answer "nothing". Instead, they are both significantly harmed.

Believe me; whatever a person may hear in a minute can take him several days, months or even years to forget. The memory may even stay with him for the rest of his life. This is all due to the "disease of talking".

A wise saint once encircled his cell many times and said, "I was just sitting amongst people, listening to them talk; but their conversation is still echoing in my ears. I need to empty my ears lest their conversation enters my cell."

St. Oar once warned his disciple saying, "my son, strange words should not enter this cell." By 'strange words' the saint was referring to any word that is not related to monasticism or is of spiritual benefit. That is, any word that does not build him spiritually. This is why a life of monasticism is different to life in the world.

In the world, a person is considered to be social if he is fluent and eloquent in his speech. Such a person is often found to keep conversations going, driving it from one subject to another. But such is not the case in monasticism. Those who talk are wasting their time, unless they are meditating on the word of God. Such talk builds the soul. It is said that St Macarius once sat with his children to talk to them and they all wept, to the extent that St Macarius drenched his beard with his tears. In this case, talking is not a harmful disease.

In the world, people love sharing stories and listening to news. They listen to the radio, read newspapers and watch television so that they can be updated with all the recent events and latest stories. However, news is not good for a monk, regardless if it is from the world, church or monastery.

A monk should care about the salvation of his soul. He should not concern himself with news. The stories he may hear may not even be true. What does a monk have to do with news? News yields thoughts which cause one to lose focus in prayer, stop meditating and waste time. It may even disturb the love one has towards his brother. Job said to his friends, "Oh, that you would be silent, and it would be your wisdom!" (Job 13:5). It is not enough for a monk to just know this verse; he needs to apply it in his life.

In the book of Genesis we read that "the serpent told [Eve]: 'Has God indeed said, "You shall not eat of every tree of the garden?"' And the woman said to the serpent, 'We may eat the fruit of the trees of the garden; but of the fruit of the tree which is in the midst of the garden, God has said, "You shall not eat it, nor shall you touch it, lest you die."' (Gen 3:1-3). Notice how precisely Eve remembered God's commandment? She did not say that God just said not to eat the fruit but "you shall not eat it, nor shall you touch it." Nevertheless, Eve touched, ate and gave the fruit to Adam.

Memorising God's commandments and verses from

the Bible is easy, but it is more important to apply them. Unfortunately, there are some people who memorise verses in order to judge others instead.

I am going to repeat my question and ask you plainly: are you building yourself every time you sit with someone in the monastery? If you are not, do not have these sittings!

Early in my monastic life, I used to lock myself in my cell and only go outside at the end of the week for prayers. I wanted to stay away from the news of the monastery. However, monks used to knock on my door and say, "Father Antonius, this happened to father so and so. We want you to pray for this matter." Therefore, I used to know what was happening in the monastery through prayer requests. I was tempted in a different way.

I felt like I was no longer confined in my cell. I felt like I was living through all the events in the monastery. Even if I was not told the whole story, the fact that I was asked to pray for a certain matter kept my mind busy with thoughts. What happened to father so and so? Is he in trouble? Should I go to his cell to know the story? Thoughts, thoughts, thoughts!

Tricks of the Devil:

The devil does not try to waste a monk's time the same way he would tempt someone living in the world. For example, the devil will not ask a monk to go to the movies. Instead, he will deceitfully try to waste his time in 'spiritual' ways such as long spiritual meetings with so called 'saints' who have died to the world. If the monk was to try to pray the psalms after a whole night wasted in such meetings, he will find his thoughts scattered. That person did this... that person said this... this happened... this didn't happen! If the monk befriends the 'saint' and spends time with him every night, he will be totally lost!

St Isaac says, "If a brother of this kind comes to you, offer him a prostration and in humility say, 'I am sorry, I have not finished my psalms yet. Let us pray together.'"

Of course, your brother did not come to pray the psalms with you and so he will probably leave. Some may argue that this might hurt the brother's feelings and that this is inappropriate in monasticism. Nevertheless, I am telling you 'live to please God', for by doing this, both of you will reap benefits. At least you are making him pray the psalms and you are completing your spiritual canon.

St Macarius the Great once said to his children as they were coming out of church, "escape my children, escape!" When they asked him what to escape from, he put his hand on his mouth and answered, "escape from this" – talking.

In the world, people say that speech is enjoyable. However, in monasticism they say that silence is comforting. In the world they say, "learn from the words of this person". However, in monasticism they say, "learn from the silence of this person". Thus, the virtues of those who live in the world are different to those in monasticism. You may say nice, comforting words to others that are full of blessing, knowledge and spirituality, but on Judgement Day God will ask you for your brother's soul if you have destroyed him your words. He will tell you, "Your brother has spent several months gathering wheat and you recklessly burned his stores."

Talking is one of the most dangerous diseases. Monks need to protect and cure themselves from this disease.

Means of Protection:

A monk can protect himself from the disease of talking by living in solitude or choosing friends who are not spiritually harmful. He may also protect himself by minding his own business or answering people briefly. For example, if someone tries to start a conversation, he could say, "the Lord will deal with the issue", "may the Lord preserve us" or "thank God". "The Paradise of the Fathers" contains many similar responses that one may use to quickly end conversations. If a monk ends the conversation his brother might leave, however some people may accuse him of not listening. In such a case, the monk should answer that he was listening and simply trying to change the subject. If he cannot do this, he should remain silent and think of another subject such that he may not delve into the first topic.

If a monk fails to end a conversation or change the subject, his brother will start explaining what happened. He may then be tempted to ask about what happened next or say, "O you reminded me of something else he did" and so they would both start talking about their brother.

I pray that the Lord may sanctify the ears and tongues of monks that He always reminds them of their aim and the reason they left the world.

In the world, stories are called "news" but in monasticism, they are called "disruptions to the community".

Regardless of the tasks he is assigned, a monk needs to be honest and ensure that he is praying as he works. Therefore, whenever people eat food or take handcraft made by a monk, they are inevitably receiving the blessings of his prayers.

A monk ought to ask himself, "Is my mind occupied with God when I work, or do I just talk and talk?" Who knows the contents of your speech? If people find out that the monk is not praying while he is working, they would stop buying anything from the monastery. Let us not forget ourselves. In monasticism, a few hours can pass like a second. All of a sudden one may realise that he has just wasted a couple of hours in worldly talk. This is a monastic calamity! Remember, a life of monasticism is different to life in the world. A monk needs to look after his time and make the most of it. He should always try to build up himself and others. He should serve in the monastery without neglecting his spirituality.

Why do we say the funeral prayers during the consecration of monks? Some people jokingly might think that they pray the funeral prayer on the white garment of a novice which then turns into the black monastic garb, as if the white clothes had died. No my beloved, these prayers are for the monk's old personality such that he may become a different person.

His thoughts are no longer like those of the people in the world.

Before monasticism, a servant may spend all his time serving. However as soon as he becomes a monk, there is no more service. A monk ought to think that he has entered the monastery to benefit from others, not the contrary. Before monasticism a person might have been a teacher, but now he is a student. He needs to try to collect anything that is useful for the salvation of his soul. Unfortunately, there are some people who join monasticism and want to educate, and share their wisdom and experiences with others. No, this is not appropriate for monasticism. If you were once a famous servant, you need to practice the life of discipleship as a monk.

Monks need to seek discipleship and try to learn something from everyone. St Anthony saw a lady who was bathing and was not ashamed of her nakedness. He listened to her words and said that it was the voice of God. St Macarius the Great learnt a lesson from a young shepherd. St Moses the Black benefited from a young boy named Zachariah. The saints always sought to hear a word of benefit and tried to apply it in their own lives. They did not distribute their wisdom or knowledge to others. You must disregard your knowledge when you become a monk.

A monk needs to ask himself, how many years have I spent in the monastery? How did I struggle to grow spiritually during this period? Have I changed? Am I living a better life? Have I grown in my knowledge? Have I gained any monastic virtues?"

It is said that monks are earthly angels. I will ask you a simple question: How far are you from becoming an earthly angel?

Have you overcome the sins you used to commit while you were in the world, or are you still the same? Do you have new faults that did not exist before? St Misael became a hermit three years after becoming a monk. What about you? How many years have passed? Have you become a hermit or an angel? Have you changed since you entered the monastery? Do you need to start again from the very beginning? Where are you now?

Recently we consecrated two new monks. I want everyone to say: 'I wish I could become a monk.' Is this a difficult statement to make? Do not say that you are already a monk and have become an elder. No, it is better to say that you wish to become a monk. When St Macarius the Great saw two hermits in the inner wilderness, he returned to his disciples and said: "I am not a monk, but I have seen monks". St Anthony also had that same feeling when he saw St Paul.

My brothers, how much have you grown in your spirituality since your monasticism? Until when will you comfort yourself and think that one becomes a monk by just wearing black garments?

True Monasticism:

Monasticism is an inner change, not an outward custom. If you read the Ladder of Divine Ascent, you will find thirty steps to monasticism. Read the book and find out how many steps you have ascended. Have you died to the world? Have you acquired the monastic virtues of asceticism, impartiality and obedience? How about the other virtues mentioned in 'The Paradise of the Fathers'?

A monk should always give a very honest account of himself. He must never justify himself but rather totally disclose his inner self. He should ask himself, "What is next? Where am I now? Where should I be? What did I gain from my monasticism? What is still left for me?" This is what St. Bishoy and St. Arsanius used to do.

Take care lest you neglect your spiritual life as the years pass by. Lest those who knew you while you were living in the world find that you are still the same person, with the same manner of speech, anger, and sensitivity. How could such a person claim that they have died to the world? Were the funeral prayers just a ritual? Mere words recited for comfort? Believe me; such a person will never reach his goal.

My dear brethren, monasticism is not about a new name and black clothes. Monasticism is a life. Consider St. Paul, who do you think prayed the consecration prayers for him? Who clothed him in the qalansuwa (head cover) or the leather girdle? St Paul did not even wear a black garment! He covered himself with palm leaves, yet he lived a true life of monasticism. St Anthony the father of all monks, called St Paul his "father"; and St Paul called St Anthony his "son". It is not a matter of clothes or appearance. Monasticism is a life.

Death to the world starts from inside the heart. During the funeral prayers, we pray that you die to the desires of the world and all its lusts. We pray that you die from your old personality, take a new name from God and start a new life.

Your brothers are not going to make you die to the world. They can pray the funeral prayers a hundred times, but nothing will happen as long as you have not died to the world from inside. It is an inner change.

A monk needs to be a blessing wherever he goes. His consecration is a blessing and a feast in the monastery. His brothers should feel his presence among them. He should be an ideal role model, an example of virtue and spiritual principles. Remember, monasticism is not just a change of clothes or a mere ritual.

Let every monk sit with himself and ask: "Am I a true monk? Am I living a true life of monasticism on the inside or from the outside only? Is monasticism my life or just a change in clothes and name? Am I dealing with daily issues with a monastic or worldly attitude?"

Monasticism is not just a change of life, but also a life of development until one reaches monastic perfection (also known as "the life of perfection").

If monasticism is a life of prayer, are you growing in your prayer? If monasticism is a life of serenity and calmness, are you growing in these virtues? If monasticism is a life of purity and holiness, have you started living in purity and holiness? If monasticism is a life of asceticism and austerity, have you started living in asceticism, loving and possessing nothing in the world? Are you at war with the desires of the flesh?

A monk may defend himself in front of others and deceive them by presenting a different image of himself.

Be honest and do not deceive yourself "For what man knows the things of a man except the spirit of the man which is in him?" (1 Cor 2:11).

Let us be honest and open with ourselves that we may evaluate our monastic life accurately, and correct our attitude and lifestyle if necessary. May the Lord, who is the examiner of our hearts and who knows our inner self, help us to live as we should through His grace.

MONASTIC RULES

History of the Monastic Rules:

Monasticism is a life with God that originally started without any rules as it is a life of solitude. Rules were applied to organise the communal life. This is why monastic rules started when monks began to live in community. St. Pakhomius established the monastic communal life and wrote the oldest monastic rules.

In the fourth century the monastic rules were transferred to St. Basil the Great the Archbishop of Caesarea, Cappadocia. He wrote monastic rules published by the Syrian monastery around 25 years ago. John Cassian transferred the rules of St. Pakhomius and St. Basil to the west. He wrote two books, 'Institutes' and 'Conferences'. In his first book he includes four chapters about monasticism, its rules and the early monastic life, while the other eight chapters are about the wars fighting the soul in a monastic way. The wars he mentioned include: gluttony, adultery, depression, anger, pride, vain glory and possession. In the collection of Nicean and Post-Nicean fathers, all eight wars were translated except the war of adultery. Maybe adultery was not translated because they were not suitable for laymen or the western way of thinking. We know that there are very strict rules for monks in fighting the wars of adultery during fasting, fighting against laziness and not seeing or meeting women, which laymen maybe could not tolerate. Perhaps this is why they were not translated.

Monastic rules were then spread into Europe, especially the 'Benedictine Monasticism' coming from the Catholic monk St. Benedict meaning 'blessed'. Then monastic groups started to establish laws for themselves. One century after St. Pakhomius, St. Shenouda the Archimandrite established more strict rules for monasticism.

In Egypt, the monastic communal life was not as successful as the life of solitude. The leadership of a monastery needs internal regulations, with a strict and spiritual person to supervise these regulations. Many monks who had abandoned the world with its leaders and regulations did not like to live the same life in monasticism. Thus, the hardest leadership is that of monks. Each one wants to live according to his own will, saying, "did I leave the world with its leaders, restrictions and regulations, to submit to leaders, restrictions and regulations in the monastery?"

That was why the monasticism of St. Pakhomius did not produce many saints. The most famous names of which we know after St. Pakhomius were, St. Petronius, St. Orothius and St. Theodore. The monasteries of St. Pakhomius had nearly vanished, but with the grace of our Lord, we revived one of them in Edfu.

The names of the mighty saints which were left for us are those of solitude. Whether from the eastern wilderness of St. Anthony, or the western wilderness of St. Makarious in Scetis or St. Amonious. We also have the host of saints who were contemporary to them and are mentioned in the Commemoration of the Saints; such as St. Bishoy, St. John the Short, St. Daniel, St. Isidore, St. Isaiah, St. Maximus and St. Domadius, St. Moses the Black, St Biemen and his brothers, St. Joseph and many other saints. They are all saints of solitude and not saints from monastic community.

There are rules for monasticism. The monk is not supposed to own anything, even his books. When a monk departs, they enter his cell and take his books to the monastery library and his utensils to the kitchen. They ask other monks if anyone needs something so that he might take it. The monk does not own his bed or his cell. As long as he has vowed poverty, how could he have possessions? Possession is against the rule of voluntary poverty.

Now from a legal point of view, the monastery inherits the monk, not his family. There is a law now that states this. Thus when a monk departs his relatives do not go and take his possessions. In the case of a priest or bishop, the church inherits him. Whatever he owns belongs to the diocese and the diocese continues after he passes away.

Before my ordination the patriarchate used to inherit the bishops, but I cancelled this system because the diocese should inherit the bishop and not the patriarchate. The amount of money for any deceased bishop was kept at his diocese. If his diocese is divided among other regions, the money is also divided because any money given to the bishop is for his diocese and its projects.

There are many monastic rules for internal regulations, especially the known rules of St. Pakhomius, St. Basil, St. Shenouda and St. Benedict. During the era of Pope Youannis the 19th who departed in 1942, he issued rules for monasticism concerning regulations for positions.

Accepting The New Monk:

The first rule in monasticism is 'accepting a new monk':

According to the rule of St. Pakhomius, a new monk should spend a testing period of three years before being consecrated as a monk. Recently the monasteries consider it a long period which many cannot tolerate, so they reduced it two years, but it was proven that the longer the testing period the better. At the convents, the testing period sometimes lasts for three, four, or even five years. There should be a lengthy period for testing.

The testing period has two sides: one from the monastery and one from the monk. The monk should examine himself, whether this type of life will be suitable for him. The monastery tests the monk whether he is appropriate to join the community of monks.

The testing period reveals the inner thoughts of the monk, so that the monastery may correct the mistakes in his personality. It also reveals whether the monk has these special three characteristics: obedience, humility and perseverance. A person who previously occupied a high position, being obeyed by everyone, may find it more challenging to demonstrate these three characteristics. He may have to obey someone younger or less educated than himself, yet he must obey to be accepted into the community of monks.

Humility can include serving everyone, and performing duties that may be unpleasant. A humble person is not annoyed when people observe him serving, or if one of his students sees himself performing laborious tasks. It is true that now many monasteries hire cleaners for the kitchen and other areas of the monastery.

Many monks today do not know about building projects, but they work as engineers or supervisors, sometimes working in the garden and the plantations of the monastery. In the older days the responsible monk was the one ploughing, planting and watering. Now there are workers for the garden, and the monk is just a supervisor rebuking and chastising the workers. This is a new problem in monasticism which never existed before.

Priesthood & Serving In The World:

Monasticism is exposed to two issues: priesthood and serving in the world. These do not concern the nuns, except the Catholic nuns.

When monasticism started, it was completely separated from priesthood. St. Pakhomius used to bring a priest from the neighbouring villages to pray the liturgy for the monks and this was the case for a long time. St. Anthony was most probably not a priest, just a monk until his departure. His disciples were among the laymen or deacons in high church positions, but he was just a monk. One of his disciples, Deacon Athanasius, became a patriarch while St. Anthony was just a monk.

St Makarious the Great was ordained a priest before his monasticism, which is very unusual. He wrote, "When I was a youth, they ordained me a priest for a village, but as I did not want it, I escaped."

Monasticism has now become so widespread and developed that even some of the monastic principles have changed. This means that the number of monks have increased dramatically. It happened that St. Isizoros was a spiritual guide for around 3000 monks. The devil was so enraged that St. Isizoros cared about one particular brother, guiding him until he prevented wars against him, that the devil said to him, "Are you not satisfied with the 3000 whom we cannot conquer, and this brother, who was our friend, you made him overcome us through your prayers?"

The numbers generally increased in thousands, even tens of thousands. It became impossible for the married priests serving in the world or the neighbouring villages to take their confessions. There was a need to ordain some of the monks as priests. For example, St. Makarious, St. Isizoros, and St. Moses the Black became priests. The number of priests increased among the monks not because they are superior than married priests, but to pastor the monks. Thus there was a need to ordain some of them as bishops.

Some of the big names in the wilderness, such as St. Daniel the father of Scetis and St. John the Short, were priests and leaders of more than 10,000 monks. Still monasticism was far away from being the head of priesthood.

At the beginning of monasticism, none of the monks were ordained as bishops or patriarchs. During the early period of Christianity, the patriarchs of Alexandria were not chosen from monasteries. They were chosen, for example, from the theological college, or from renowned deacons such as Athanasius the 20th pope. Another example of a patriarch not chosen from a monastery was Pope Demetrius the vinedresser, who was just a simple kind hearted layman. What is really strange is that this simple man, through the Holy Spirit dwelling in him, was able to confront the greatest theologian of that age and excommunicate him for his theological mistakes. That person was Origen, the lecturer and dean of the theological College, the greatest teacher who advanced far greater in knowledge than the bishops of the world.

Some say that the first patriarch ordained from monks in Egypt was Pope Cyril the Great. This is uncertain as his uncle was Pope Theophilus the 23rd. It was him who sent Pope Cyril to the monastery for a while who then came back and became his personal secretary. Was he then actually consecrated as a monk or did he just spend a retreat period in the monastery like Athanasius when he used to spend time with St. Anthony? His monasticism is uncertain.

When the greatest teacher of his age Habib Girgis was nominated he was an archdeacon, and in the history of the church many popes and bishops were originally deacons. He was an archdeacon and the Dean of the Theological College. They refused his nomination for the Giza Diocese, considering him a layman, while in church rites an archdeacon is not a layman.

The same case with Wadie Saeid, who later became Fr. Daoud El Maqari. They refused him more than once to be ordained as a bishop. Finally, he was to be consecrated as a monk in St. Makarious monastery as Fr. Daoud El Maqari, however when he was a layman his nomination as bishop was rejected.

Another example is Gabriel Ibn Turik, who was Abul Alaa Ibn Turik. When he was a layman he was nominated for the Papacy. Thus they took him at night and consecrated him as a monk, and then ordained him a priest in 'The Hanging Church'. They then sent him to Alexandria to be ordained as patriarch. These are all formalities, exactly like putting on the Eskeem.

The early canons of monasticism state that a monk should be a full time worshipper, praying, meditating and living in solitude, thus appearing to represent the most suitable candidates for the patriarchate. Yet we found that the Coptic Church on many occasions ordained popes not from among monks, such as pope Abraam Ibn Zaraa. During his era in the 10th century the Muqqatam Mountain was moved. He was a simple merchant, yet he was ordained as a pope.

During the period of Pope Cyril, who was considered a monk from St. Makarious monastery until Pope Benjamin the 38th pope, only five of them were monks. A number of people consider that the first pope to be ordained among monks was Pope Youannis I (the 29th pope). These five were chosen from St. Makarious monastery, the Zugag monastery, Tabor monastery and Cyprian or Keprios monastery.

The papacy began to be settled through the choosing of monks since the 40th pope, who was chosen from St. Makarious monastery. Since then, the monks were the ones ordained for higher clerical positions as bishop or patriarch. Even if there is an appropriate person for papacy who is not a monk, he has to be ordained as a monk first.

The monks who are ordained bishops or patriarchs cannot at all live according to the original rites of monasticism. They cannot truly live in solitude, silence, worship and meditation, no matter how hard they try. Total honesty for pastorship does not give sufficient time for solitude, quietness, worship and meditation. If they live in solitude for worship and meditation, they will not be able to fulfil the commitments of pastorship.

Before my ordination as a pope, they used to celebrate clothing the new bishop in the Eskeem on the day of his ordination. I found that it was impossible for a bishop to fulfil the duties of the Eskeem; it was just formalities and external procedures, so we cancelled wearing the Eskeem to avoid loading the bishop with more bondage. We were loading them with duties and a certain spiritual position which they cannot perform. The ordained bishop cannot go for a retreat or live in solitude and silence. He has certain duties to perform as a bishop and his life style completely changes.

Recluses:

Why don't we establish monasteries for the recluses?

If we establish a monastery for the original monasticism and recluses, shall we allow people to visit or not? If we allow visits, then the monastery will be full of visitors. In this case, the monk did not go to the world but the world came to him. The visitors will like the quiet recluses, and if there is a need to ordain a bishop, they will choose one of them.

Special monasteries for recluses could be built far from the monastery where no laymen are allowed to visit. They should be under a spiritual leader who is not in the form of an abbot or bishop. As for the place, we suggest the deserted monasteries in Scetis wilderness, such as St. John the short monastery.

In the wilderness of Scetis there are remnants of Monasteries that are empty and deserted. Prince Omar Toson marked them with pieces of copper to indicate that they were monasteries. The Arabs in the desert took these copper pieces with some writings, and excavations should be done there.

Going back to the question; why don't we establish monasteries for the recluses? There is a contradiction in this question. Seclusion is one thing and monasteries are another thing. The recluses do not live in monasteries, but in isolated areas, such as caves, holes in the mountains, and scattered cells in the wilderness. If they live in a monastery, they are monks in a monastery and not recluses.

In the past the monks needed the laymen. When the monks used to weave baskets, they needed the laymen to sell their products to them, or else they would have to go to the city themselves, which for them was far worse!

There are jobs in the monastery that need laymen, such as building of the cells, digging a well to get water in the monastery, fixing the water wells...etc.

The ideal scenario for these monks is living in caves up the mountains. In this case, there is no monastery or leadership, and this exists at present. Any monk who wants to become a recluse is advised to go and live in the mountain, but a recluse monk living in the communal life of the monastery is a contradiction. Referring to the previous question, maybe we can have a monastery with monks who are not recluses but far from the noisy world and contact with laymen.

If more than one monk is staying in a place, it is not secluded place anymore. St. Isaac said, "If you are living with one, you are called the second, if you are living with two, you are called the third, and if you are living with three you are called the fourth. You can never be called a recluse unless you live alone."

Do not think that staying away from people is only being away from laymen. It also involves staying away from monks, and maybe in monasticism it is even better to stay away from monks than to stay away from laymen. It is more dangerous and requires greater caution if you are closer to the monks than the laymen. Why is this the case? The layman who comes to the monastery is looking for quality spiritual time. He comes with great enthusiasm. He sits with the monks and talks about spiritual matters, or receives a word of benefit for his salvation. However a monk who is used to much talking might sit with another monk for long periods about non-spiritual matters, and this negatively affects him. Therefore, seclusion in the proper context of monasticism is for monks to stay away from everyone.

St. Isaac wrote about seclusion more than any other person. He was a recluse and his brother St. Matthew was the Abbot of a monastery in the Sinai close to Syria. When St. Matthew invited St. Isaac to come and visit the monastery, he replied with a message saying, "Maybe my brother you do not care for the salvation of my soul, how could I then come to the monastery? Of course these are very humble words, but seclusion is what it is.

If the recluses gathered in a monastery, they will need laymen for building the monastery's services. This would lead to the monastery serving the laymen by allowing visits and overnight stays. If the monastery does not serve them, they will be upset and cause problems. If the monastery catered for some people and did not cater for others, there would be reproach and anger. If no one is allowed to visit at all, the everyday needs of life such as food and drink would be affected. Therefore combining the two issues is a problem.

He who wants seclusion should go and live in a cave in the mountains. If he does not want to meet anyone, he should keep his cave unknown and not meet anyone. As for his needs, they should be met through one of his spiritual disciples in the monastery, going weekly or every couple of weeks to deliver his need according to a certain rule. It is known that only one person should serve the recluse, as both have a common understanding. However if the person serving the recluse starts disrupting his seclusion he might change the person, but this may not solve the problem due to the insistence of laymen visiting and disrupting their time.

One of the priests who departed while I was a bishop in the Theological College wanted to see me. I used to lock myself in my cell on Friday to prepare the weekly lecture. When others told him that I cannot meet him, he insisted to come up to my room and kept knocking strongly on my door, but I refused to open the door.

During the days of St. Anthony there were also people who did not respect the privacy of a monk. After St. Anthony spent 30 years as a recluse, the laymen insisted on meeting him and broke his door. Their persistence resulted in St Anthony leaving his secluded place and guiding future monks, when they said to him, "Guide us and we will become your disciples." Thus he became the father of monks.

It happened that some laymen gathered in front of the door of a recluse and kept saying "Lord have mercy", but he did not open. Some went on to say that the Lord Jesus Himself said, "Knock and it will be open to you" (Matt.7: 7), while they do not open for us. They might send harsh letters and say unkind words. They may even hear someone saying, 'this is not a monastery for the recluses, only a monastery for the haughty ones.' This is a hard stumbling block, and finally the recluse might be urged to meet whoever comes to him.

When pope Theophilus wanted to visit St Arsanius he replied, "If I meet you, then I will meet everyone, and if I meet everyone I cannot live in this place anymore." So the pope said, "If we go to him, it is like we are dismissing him from that place" and he never went to him.

In such a monastery, if a bishop comes to visit, would they meet him or not? If yes, then all those accompanying the bishop would also come in with him. If not, it will be an Ecclesiastical problem; he might even accompany a different group each time. Thus the monastery would be full of laymen, in addition to the families of the monks.

This is another issue: are the recluses allowed to meet their families? One person might agree to meet their family while another might refuse.

I might be here in the monastery, too busy with meetings and appointments and someone might say, 'I will commit suicide if I do not see him now'. Sometimes the visitor might get angry and start shouting.

A sick person who has no hope of recovery might come to the monastery of the recluses to pray for him. He may be carried by a group of people to reach the monastery. Would the monastery allow them in or not? Alternatively, people might come hoping to meet the recluses and benefit from them, but when faced with the refusal to enter they will go back broken hearted. They will say that Christ said, "I was sick and you visited

Me." (Matt 25: 36). We came to your door, it is not you who came to us, and now then you do not want to let us in! It is not an easy matter.

Poverty & Chastity:

The rule for a monk is that he is not supposed to own any money. He only has the right to use whatever is in his cell but not to own it. The monastery provides him with a furnished room and necessities so that he does not bring his own furniture. If a monk gets angry that he does not own these things, or that the monastery takes these things away from him, then he has lost the vow of voluntary poverty.

This poverty starts at the very beginning of his monasticism and draws upon the fact that St. Anthony left all his possessions and became a monk.

There is a question in the canons of St. Basil: is it correct for a monk to give his money to his relatives before becoming a monk? We have many rules for this issue, some monks accept it, and others do not. In fact the matter goes according to the legal rules of inheritance.

We have to differentiate between the monastic rule and the civil rule of ownership. In the monastic rule the monk does not own and inherit anything, but according to the civil rule he inherits. If he inherits anything, he can send the inheritance to the monastery, but if he keeps it the monastery cannot take it off him. If that is the case then legally it is the monastery's right to dismiss the monk because he has breached one of the vows of monasticism, that is, voluntary poverty. In that case, he will go out claiming that the monastery wants to take his possessions, while the Holy Bible says, "Go your way, sell whatever you have and give to the poor." (Mark 10: 21).

That monk might cause troubles for the monastery. If he is asked who are the poor whom you want to give your money to he would answer 'the Lord commands us to give secretly, I am not telling you who these poor people are.' He can give a 'spiritual' answer to avoid facing the truth.

The monk does not have the right to own possessions, even if the aim is giving to the poor. The mere owning of something means that he has breached the vow of monasticism. He cannot own something under the name of virtue. St. Isaac says, "If you were told this is a good deed, your answer should be 'I know it is a good deed, but I do not want it for the sake of God."

It is not appropriate that one virtue destroys another. It is written in The Paradise of the Monks concerning clothes that the monk should not have more than two robes. One robe is being worn while the other is being washed. Monks should not value clothes to the extent that if a monk were to throw his robe outside his cell for days, no one would take it following the rule of poverty which he has vowed.

This is an important rule of monasticism, to have no possessions. St. Basil the Great was asked, 'Is it okay for a monk to leave some things and keep other things for himself?' So he answered, "It is written that all who believed were together, and had all things in common, so whoever says that he owns something becomes a stranger in the Church of God".

If there is a true life of community, like the era of the Apostles, each one would sell their possessions and goods, dividing them among all as anyone had need. If someone were to say 'this is mine' it would be wrong. The system was that all the money should go to the Apostles. They gave each one according to his needs. Nobody owned and fell short of anything. Maybe this was where the word 'Communism' came from.

Thus, all the rules of monasticism include no possessions or poverty. This is a monastic step mentioned in St. John Climacus' book, 'The ladder of Divine Ascent'.

Poverty also includes asceticism, which is related to the heart more than anything else. A monk is an ascetic person living in poverty and not owning anything, but rather giving in everything.

In monasticism, celibacy is a condition of the life of chastity, yet some who were not celibates joined monasticism. These may have been either widows or people who agreed with their wives to live in chastity. In such a case where the husband and wife agree to live as monastics, the husband goes to the monastery, and the woman goes to the convent or a similar consecrated house.

Some people who have left their wives and became monks include St. Paul the Simple who when his wife fell in sin, left her and became a monk. The married couple should both approve on such a situation, and the church should authorise it. Another example is Father Amonious of the Niteria Mountain who was forced into marriage and lived for 18 years in celibacy with his wife. She then said to him, "It is better for you to become a monk because you cannot live this life as a married man."

Another principal concerning chastity for monks is staying away from women. St. Basil was so strict in this issue. He said among his canons, "If there is an urgent need to meet a woman, the monk should only discuss this matter quickly with her, and be accompanied with the attendance of another person." The same was said concerning meeting nuns, "If there were an urgent need, more than one monk would go and return quickly."

Life of Continuous Prayer

Monastic life above everything is a life of continuous prayer. A layman can do everything that a monk does, except continuous prayer. This is the major difference between a monk and a layman because continuous prayer involves no distractions and laymen do not have this luxury. The monk's entire life is dedicated to God. Laymen are able to perform merciful deeds, and educate and serve others, but one thing they cannot achieve is continuous prayer.

Monks are called 'earthly angels' for two reasons:

1- Striving for purity of the heart

2- Striving to pray continuously

Those who joined monasticism become monks

mainly for the life of continuous prayer. This is why monks live in solitude. Of course solitude is not the aim in itself, but it is a means to reach continuous prayer. St. Arsanius used to avoid even meeting saints. When St. Makarious the Alexandrian asked him, "Why are you avoiding us, my father?" He replied, "I cannot talk to people and God at the same time." Those who want to reach total consecration for prayer with God, let them live in solitude and quietness.

Also silence in itself was not an intended virtue but a means to reach continuous prayer. When people practice silence, it is not to reach the virtue of silence, but to keep the mind busy with God. A spiritual elder once said 'he who talks much is empty from inside', meaning that he is empty from continuous prayer.

The fathers lived in the wilderness and deserts for the sake of mastering continuous prayer. They then entered into the inner wilderness to give all their time to God. To achieve continuous prayer, they kept protecting their senses. We know that this is a virtue because the senses bind the thoughts. We think about what we see and hear, and act on them. The senses are the gates of the mind, and to be at peace concerning our thoughts we have to control our senses. The question is 'why do we have to control our thoughts to live at peace'? It is in order to keep the mind thinking about God. Thus for the sake of continuous prayer they preserved their senses.

Most of the monk's readings are to consecrate the heart for continuous prayer. Therefore we aim to choose the readings which help in prayer, or which give us fiery prayer. Not everything is beneficial to read for the monk who wants to achieve a continuous connection with God. He has to read until his feelings yearn for God, then he will start praying.

Continuous prayer is an expression of the love of a person and the relationship to God. When we love someone we think about them much. When you love God you will think of Him and be busy with Him. The person who does not pray much does not love God much. The more love we have for God the more we will pray. Therefore, if we say that solitude and silence is a means to God, which helps prayer, then we say that prayers are an expression of our love to God.

There are many stories about the prayers of monks. We recall them to see how they would affect us. St. Arsanius used to spend the whole night in prayer, facing the east with the sun behind him, and he kept praying until the sun was facing him and shining once again. St. Bishoy used to stay awake all night praying, tying his hair lest he should slumber or sleep. St. Makarious

of Alexandria crucified his mind in God. He said to his
mind, "Be still there, you have God, the angels and the
saints, and do not come out of the cycle". He kept doing
this practice for four days.

The saints used to work all day while praying
continuously. One of the saints said, "Prayers for them
are like a breath coming in and out."

Prayers for the saints were lengthy, deep and full
of quality. It was not just a matter of spending time in
prayer, but praying deeply in reverence, in humility,
with concentration, with love, faith, understanding,
and meditation. These prayers were turned into visions;
the mind being occupied with God unaware of its
surroundings and opening the gates of heaven to work
miracles.

The people of the world are all specialised in a
specific skill which they master. Likewise the monks are
specialised in the skill of prayer. We do not approach
monks because they are intelligent or knowledgeable for
there are many intelligent and knowledgeable people
in the world. We approach monks because of their
skill in prayer. People view a monk as an angel who
has a strong relationship with God, and He accepts his
prayers. If they find a monk who does not pray without
ceasing, he might be a stumbling block for them.

Prayers also purify the mind and heart of a monk, as well as sanctify his mind. Anything we hear, read or think about affects us. The status of our heart depends on our thoughts. If we are thinking about the world, our heart will be connected to the world. If we are thinking of sin, then our heart will be inclined towards sin. If our heart is connected to God, our thoughts will also be connected to God. The heart and the mind are walking together. The more we occupy our mind with prayers, the less chance it has to think about the world.

Those who decrease or get lazy in their prayers may be fought with evil thoughts that affect them, as the saying goes, 'a lazy mind is a laboratory for the devil'. Devils will throw these people everywhere, because they will find the house empty and ready for any devil to dwell inside it.

Many spiritual fathers cured their spiritual problems with prayer. The more a person prays the more his mind will be clinging to God. He will have no time to think about sin as he is too busy with God. No time to think about anything else or any problem.

We know the story of St. John the Short who was always thinking about God. He was so intent on the things of God that he became very absent minded. One day when a person knocked at his door three times to carry away his materials and tools to another place, he forgot what he went inside for till he repeated to himself, "The camel, my tools. The camel and my tools. The camel, my tools." If a person becomes occupied with God, they can never think of anything else. They will forget their problems, their sins, their evil thoughts, the thoughts of the world, the problems of others and so on. All of these will vanish since there is no time for them.

Is it possible for the devil to fight you with the sin, to avenge or judge others while you are praying? No! You are too busy with God. The devil will knock on the door of your heart but he will find you busy.

Prayer is a medicine and a cure for the evil thoughts. It purifies the heart and thus prayer also is connected to the life of repentance. St. Isaac says, "Whoever thinks that there is another way for repentance except by prayer is deceived by the devils". This is true for two reasons: one is that the mind is occupied with God, living in repentance and not having time for sin. The other is that through prayer we gain a divine support aiding us in repentance.

Prayer is a virtue in this field. Your mind will be ashamed to think about something evil after prayer, after you were just talking with God. It is similar when a person is ashamed to sin after receiving Holy Communion. Not praying or neglecting prayer will open the door for the enemy. When the person sins he has forgotten God. A praying person remembers God, He is before their eyes at all times. Thus the life of prayer leads him to the life of purity and repentance.

Believe me, prayer will teach us all virtues. If we meditate on the words of the Agpia prayers for example, we will find in them all kinds of virtues. Even in the prayer "Our Father Who art in Heaven", we will find a spiritual path open before us. Prayer helps in meditation, and meditation helps in prayer. Thus both of these help in the life of virtue; we need only to apply them.

It is enough to tell Him in your prayer, 'O Lord, teach me Your ways, let me understand Your paths, teach me the way which I should walk through'. In prayer ask God to accompany you. Thus continuous prayer is communion with God. It is a friendship and companionship, being always in the Divine presence.

In intermittent prayers, a person may build and then fall. He builds his spirituality during prayer, and then because he neglects prayer for a long time he will lose what he has already built. He keeps building and falling, without any consistency.

A wonderful word said by St. John El Tabaysy when they asked him, 'what is continuous prayer?' He answered, "It is death from the world". If a person is continuously praying the world is not inside his heart any more. It is real death to the world because prayer does not give any chance to become connected to anything in the world.

It is said, 'Monasticism is giving up everything to become connected to the One'. When we are connected to the One in continuous prayer, we are giving up everyone and everything. It is inappropriate while praying to be connected to others or certain issues; otherwise our prayer would be without concentration.

Continuous prayer is death to the world. If we think about the world while praying, then we are going back to it. Some of us might ask, there are many stories of saints and many sayings by the fathers about continuous prayer but how can we reach it? We cannot reach it in one step, but let us start in the path and then we will develop.

Let us not think that the seven prayers in the Agpia are the only canon in our prayers. These prayers are the duty of all Christians living in the world who are working, and who are even married. They all should pray the seven prayers of the Agpia.

The first person who prayed the seven prayers was a married man, David the Prophet. He says "seven times a day I praise You, because of Your righteous judgments." (Ps. 119:164). The Agpia prayers are for all Christians, but continuous prayers are for the monks. We should have a prayer schedule, greater and stronger than the Agpia prayers. It is a good idea to memorise prayers, such as other psalms not mentioned in the Agpia. There are also many resources on prayer, such as the prayers of the saints, the numerous praises in the Apocalypses Vigil, and other books specifically dedicated to praises. Therefore, we should read and learn how to pray continuously.

A monk should pray as much as he can in his leisure time. He should also mix every work with prayer. Any job in the monastery or any spiritual work by the monk should be mixed with prayer. He should not allow long periods of the day without prayer, even if it is the use of short repeated prayers. He should raise his mind to God continuously through the saying of a short sentence, really putting prayer in front of his eyes at all times.

Let us mention two verses from the Holy Bible:

"men always ought to pray and not to lose heart." (Luke 18: 1).

"Pray without ceasing." (1 Thes 5: 17).

If these commandments are given to Christians in general, how much more so for monks? Which one of us has fulfilled these verses?

If we know how to pray continuously let us not fall into vain glory. If we pray all our psalms and the Agpia Prayers, let us tell ourselves, 'I still have a lot to do, I have to pray without ceasing.'

BALANCE

Many monks go to the extreme in their spiritual life. However, monasticism requires a balance in many aspects of one's life.

Freedom:

What is freedom? People often think that monasticism is a life of freedom, without any pressures or urgent matters. However freedom may lead to lawlessness. In such a case a monk ignores the rules of the monastery and does whatever he wants. He may ignore the sound of the monastery's bell and come to prayer or the refectory whenever he wishes. Such a monk may even fight with his brothers for not asking about him whenever he does not attend.

Freedom does not involve breaking free of the monastery's system and disobeying its rules. Some monks think they can enjoy freedom by doing whatever they want whenever they want or by not following the system of the monastery. However, true freedom is experienced on the inside. It is the ability to have self-control and remove bad habits. Freedom can also be acquired when one frees himself from the authority of his ego.

It is easy for a person who follows the monastery's system and obeys its rules to carry out God's commandments. But if someone cannot obey in small things, how can he obey difficult things? If a monk does not want to follow a particular system, he needs to speak to the person responsible and frankly explain to him why he perceives the system to be inappropriate. However as long as he accepts a system, he needs to commit to it.

Monks living in solitude are exempt from the services of the community. However, such monks are expected to abide by the rules of solitude and not live in a state of lawlessness. They must not mingle with others and engage in politics or worldly issues. Instead they must live in complete silence in continuous prayer and asceticism appropriate for seclusion.

Controlling The Tongue:

Some monks may be completely silent, while others may talk much without any restrictions or limits. However, there needs to be a balance between talking and being silent.

The first step in controlling the tongue involves abstaining from the sins of the tongue. Once accomplished, a monk ought to keep his tongue from talking about trivial matters or issues that do not concern his salvation. As he grows in this virtue, he ought to think and only speak when necessary so that his words may be of benefit and edification. He should then think about how he can speak little, yet sufficient words.

When silent, a monk should be praying and meditating silently so that he does not feel like he is better than others. When one is busy talking to God, he is not talking to people.

Eating And Fasting:

A balance is also required between eating and fasting. Some people strictly fast during the Holy Lent but eat as much as they desire during the holy fifty days. In such cases, the asceticism that was gained during the Holy Lent is lost with the joys of the Resurrection.

How can one achieve a balance during the holy fifty days between self-control and bodily desires? How can a monk or ascetic rejoice without returning to the lifestyle of a layman? A monk ought to rejoice without fasting, but with self-control. They must be careful not to indulge in food without self-control, especially after much abstinence during holy week.

The transition between the Holy Lent and the holy fifty days is not the only problem. Saturdays and Sundays are also joyful days, without prostrations or abstinence. How can one live in lawlessness during these two days and lose whatever he has gained throughout the past five days? We need to be careful and try to achieve a balance in our spiritual life.

Monks need to sit with their confession father and agree upon a system to follow. The monk who honestly discusses his situation and level of spirituality with his spiritual father is wise. However, he who keeps building and falling is not benefiting very much from his monasticism.

Prayer:

Concerning prayer, I love the words of St Isaac, "You will never reap fruits for unstable work". This implies that one cannot reap the fruits of a virtue if he is not consistent in his struggle. Someone once said, "Consistent little things are better than large interrupted things." Therefore, a person who follows a clear and gradual system (for example, one who starts reciting a few short prayers and then gradually increasing them) is better than he who starts praying for several hours and then shortens his prayers. He may then go back to increasing his prayers, but then decrease them again, not following a stable system. If you were to ask such a person about his spiritual life, he would never know where he is or what is included in his spiritual canon. Some people think that living without a system or canon is the freedom of the Holy Spirit which guides them according to the situation. No, God never said that.

In the miracle of the five loaves and two fish, Christ said, "Make them sit down in groups of fifty" (Luke 9:14) and "So they sat down in ranks, in hundreds and in fifties" (Mark 6:40). The Gospels clearly mention that the people were sitting in groups and the food was distributed in an organised manner. Christ gave food to the disciples, and the disciples passed it on to others until it reached all the people. Even when they collected the leftovers there was order – twelve baskets for the twelve disciples. St Paul states, "Let all things be done decently and in order" and "the rest I will set in order when I come." (1 Cor 11:34).

God created the stars, planets and universe in order. He created the human body with amazing systems. Plants and animals also operate in natural systems. Therefore it is very hard to believe that God would make the Holy Spirit work in our lives in a chaotic or disorganised manner. God's providence is wonderful through the work of the Holy Spirit.

Some people misinterpret the word "without law" (1 Cor 9:21) as not being under the law but under grace. However, St Paul does not mean that "those who are without law" are not following a certain order or commandment. There is a difference between being above the law and not being bound by any law.

For example, a person who generously gives his money to the poor is not bound by the tithes. Such a person is not under the law, but above the level of the tithes. Another example is someone who fasts the whole week. He is not limited to just fasting on Wednesdays and Fridays, and is therefore above the level of the law. The same applies to the one who has reached the level of divine love; above the literal meaning of the commandment to love. Thus St Augustine said, "Love first, then do whatever you want" because love is a higher level than the commandment. One may say that he is bound to thousands of commandments, but the truth is that he is not bound to these commandments as long as he has the divine love. Then all matters will correctly fall into place. Again, a person who prays without ceasing is not bound to a law that states that he must pray a certain number of psalms every hour, because he is above that law. Yet, some fathers say that even those who pray continuously need to pray the psalms. Therefore, "without law" does not refer to one who lives in lawlessness or without any commitment, but rather those who have reached a higher level, above the general commandment that applies to everyone.

True freedom is a life of perfection; free from worldly desires and fear. He who lives in this freedom does not need commandments because he is already fulfilling more than the commandments. There is a saying that if one wants to deliver a message he ought to send a wise man without commanding him. A wise man does not need a law because his wisdom will guide him – he has already reached a level that surpasses the commandment. However, a person who sins is in need of the commandment.

Commitment:

Commitment requires obedience, humility and respect. If a monk claims that he cannot attend the midnight prayers because he was praying all night and happened to sleep an hour before the midnight bell, he is excused. However, if a monk spends the night in idle talk, engaging in non-spiritual matters and can barely finish his psalms or prostrations, he will need to attend the midnight prayers.

Believe me, the most productive days are those in which we attend the midnight prayers. But the one who hears the bell ringing at midnight and has not completed his canon, or chooses to pray the midnight praise in his cell, is delinquent in his spiritualty and the order of the monastery. He is also a bad role model for others.

Satan often disguises sin in sheepskin and gives them names so that they do not appear to be sin. For example, he may depict lawlessness, disobedience, and rebellion as "the glorious liberty of the children of God". But does this really mean that the children of God are living in righteousness, holiness, prayer and virtue? Or is it referring to freedom from sin? We have to understand this properly. We are supposed to be free from sin, not virtue. If vigilance is a virtue, then not being vigilant is a sin.

Satan can also deceive a person by saying, "If the Son makes you free, you shall be free indeed." (John 8:36). Here St. John is talking about freedom from weaknesses and evil desires – not righteousness and order. We need to understand the true meaning of liberty which lifts us up and helps us draw near to God, not the liberty which pulls us away from God and makes us delinquent in everything.

Judging:

Many monks do not have a balance in their judgements. They judge others very strictly, sometimes even harshly, but judge themselves in a lenient manner often justifying their mistakes. When are we going to practice the contrary? When are we going to judge others with kindness and judge ourselves strictly? When will we seek goodness from ourselves before seeking it in others? When will we excuse others before excusing ourselves? When will we take out the plank in our own eyes before criticising others for the speck in their eyes? There needs to be a balance in our lives such that we may live in truth.

An abbot might have a certain way of thinking, while a monk under his guidance may have a different way of thinking. For example, a monk may hear a loud noise in his cell and get annoyed at his brother as he perceives such noise as inappropriate in the monastery. However that same monk may walk in the monastery and call out to someone with a loud voice, without even realising it. In such a case, the monk has no balance between his thoughts and behaviour inside and outside his cell.

A monk needs to be the same person and not adopt two different personalities. It is strange how many monks talk about attaining great virtues (such as silence, asceticism, and continuous prayer), without perfecting basic virtues (such as obedience and humility). For example, a monk may talk about the grace that allows him to pray without ceasing, however he is unable to control his anger. Such a monk may have no tolerance for others. If his brothers' words or behaviour are contrary to his methods, he would be troubled. But what is harder: continuous prayer or self-control? Of course, controlling one's temper is easier! Yet it is easy for a person to say that this monk has great virtues when he cannot attain basic virtues.

A monk may ask "what does it mean to control one's senses"? They used to tell us to control our senses when we were young, yet a monk may not be able to control his senses outside his cell. Thus, the virtue that a monk thought was minor actually requires much effort to attain.

We need to know our weaknesses and struggle to remove them. Removing our sins is one thing, while escaping them is another thing. One might refrain from communicating with others in order to avoid falling into the sin of anger. Such a person is escaping from anger but has not overcome the sin. Whenever he is faced with anything that irritates him, he will lose his temper and get angry. Another person may try to avoid situations where he will be proud. However, whenever he is exposed to any of these situations his pride will surface. Therefore, removing a sin is different to escaping from it. It is true that sometimes escaping helps us remove our sins; however it is not always the case.

A monk might say, "I am escaping big responsibilities to escape from being proud", but there may be many other reasons for being proud in his thoughts and feelings which he is not disclosing. It is not a matter of escaping but struggling against sin. Are the saints in a state of escape or freedom? One may be in a state of escape out of fear of falling into sin. However, freedom means that one will not fall into sin, even in the face of the harshest temptations.

The Life of Discipline

In the pages to follow we will aim to talk about the life of discipline, how a person should be disciplined in his life, his attitude and relationships. A disciplined person should also be honest in his dealings with God, people and himself.

Dealing With One's Self:

Each person should be disciplined in honesty. It may be easy for a person to be disciplined in his private cell where no one can see him, and to be disciplined in front of people because by our nature we want to look perfect in front of others not being exposed or criticised, lest people see our weaknesses and mistakes. If we do this we might be reflecting an inaccurate state inside.

Here I would like to touch on a brief point which we

shall revisit later; there is a difference between discipline and being legalistic. A person might be disciplined to the level of legalism where he perceives faults that are not really faults. A person may also exaggerate mistakes more than their actual size, and may even possibly become a Pharisee living according to the word! When we talk about discipline we do not mean these types of people.

Discipline is a moderate state which does not deviate to the left into legalism or to the right into irresponsibility. Discipline means that a person should stay away from laziness and irresponsibility, while examining and controlling himself.

A disciplined person would be well organised in having appointments and managing their time. He would not permit wasting one minute of his time, and he would also care for other people's time. Generally speaking if a person is prone to wasting his own time, then it would be easy for him to waste other people's time since he thinks that time does not really matter for them.

A disciplined person would also be disciplined in his thoughts. He would not allow any vain thought in his mind. You may ask 'what is the difference between a wrong thought and a vain one'? Quite simply a wrong thought can be like a thought of sin, but a vain thought is thinking of something without benefit, such as a person looking and focusing on the building structure of his cell. The same applies to talking; there is sinful speech and vain speech.

A disciplined person thinks about his words, every word should have a meaning or an aim. It may happen that someone might say something inappropriate, and when blamed for it he might say 'I didn't mean it' because he was not disciplined. Therefore we have to choose our words carefully.

A few of the things which prevent discipline is rushing into speaking, giving opinions and judging others. He who slows down and considers his words before saying them will be more disciplined. The Apostle says, "Let every man be swift to hear, slow to speak, slow to wrath..." (James 1: 19). 'Slow to speak' does not mean that he does not know how to speak, but rather to think of the meaning of the words before speaking.

There is also a person who speaks and then after thinking of his words, would not repeat what he had said. People may also judge him after he spoke. Thus one should judge himself before speaking, giving himself the chance to change or alter his words.

A disciplined person also sets a guard over the tone of his voice. It is not higher or lower than necessary, thus he speaks calmly. There is a person with a loud voice which can be irritating, yet he does not care as he is not disciplined. This is especially true at night in the monastery where voices echo or when one is repairing something in his cell at night.

A disciplined person watches carefully over his attitude and its effect on others, whether it is appropriate or inappropriate. The Apostle says: "All things are lawful for me, but not all things edify" (1 Cor 10:23). Thus there are lawful things that can be inappropriate. For example food in itself is not a sin, yet it is inappropriate to eat without self-control.

A disciplined person also takes care even while walking or standing with others. The spiritual fathers portray it as: 'opening and closing the door gently', i.e. the person takes care to not make any noise while moving around.

A disciplined person is ideal in all his attitudes. He is ideal in his general life and also upon entering the church. A disciplined person would say: "But as for me, I will come into Your house in the multitude of Your mercy; In fear of You I will worship toward Your holy temple" (Ps 5:7). He enters the church with awe. Even the removing of our shoes at the door of the church shows that we have to be very disciplined when entering such a holy place. Walking inside the church should be slow and without running. Also standing and sitting in the church should be with discipline.

There is also discipline in prayer. There is a type of person who would rush into prayer, not understand what he is saying. There is another type praying slowly and understanding the meaning of each word he says.

A disciplined person is not swayed by any passing thought. He has a strong and disciplined personality. He does not forget himself. He maintains his principles and values, which he keeps diligently and never undermines them. He performs every deed diligently. Let us go through a simple example; we all sign the cross, yet does each of us sign the cross with appropriate respect for the cross? Do we understand the meaning concerning the special doctrine of the Trinity, Incarnation and the work of the Holy Spirit, or is it just an action performed without discipline, understanding and reverence?

A disciplined person is also disciplined in his confessions. He is cautious about the sins which are clothed in sheep's clothing taking the form of a virtue while it is a sin.

Discipline involves assessing each word and its meaning. A disciplined person ensures that the means are appropriate for the aim. He does not choose the wrong means for good intentions.

There are limits to each attitude. If a person is joking, he has to be cautious so that he does not taunt people, and say hurting words to others. He laughs with people, not at people. It happens that people offend others while joking, or they hurt them unintentionally because there is a lack of discipline. He might say a joke without knowing its effect on others.

A disciplined person chooses his words. Our Lord Jesus Christ warned us about the word 'Raca' and 'fool' saying, "But whoever says, 'You fool!' shall be in danger of hell fire." (Matt 5: 22). How many times does a person use the word 'fool' with all its synonyms? He may say this person is stupid and has no mind.' These are all synonyms of the word 'fool'. Christ chose very gentle words in His conversation with the Samaritan Woman. Very tender words although she was a sinner!

A disciplined person also does not justify his behaviour regardless of the effects. Justifying is against discipline. He should make excuses for himself. Unfortunately, there are many people who are strict when criticising others, but not with themselves. They are so strict with others, but very soft with themselves. Indeed the contrary should apply. One should give an account of himself with honesty and discipline, without excuse. As for others, try to justify or make excuses for them. We notice that our Lord Jesus Christ has given us a good example. He said "how can you say to your brother, 'Let me remove the speck from your eye'; and look, a plank is in your own eye?" (Matt 7:4). This gives rise to the need to be disciplined in giving a self-account, while being gentle in criticising others.

An obstacle in the life of discipline is that sometimes we divide our sins into minor and major. We are lenient in small issues, but a disciplined person knows that every sin has the possibility to destroy, no matter how small it may seem. Any small fault can cause harm. If there is a small cut in your clothes you cannot wear it because it is torn. If a robe has only one stain, it ruins it. Even one microbe in food can be harmful.

A disciplined person aims at perfection, never justifying or excusing himself. He is disciplined with any responsibility delegated to him. If he needs to make a decision, he discerns between his responsibility and authority.

He does not justify his mistakes by giving excuses, but is earnest with all that he has. He does his best to aim for perfection. He does not say "my circumstances are not helping me to say more than two Psalms." Indeed, one should try and organise his routine or improve his circumstances to live in discipline.

A disciplined person does not wait until he falls into the depth of sin. He is disciplined and cautious from the beginning, remembering the verse "O daughter of Babylon, who are to be destroyed, happy the one who repays you as you have served us! Happy the one who takes and dashes your little ones against the rock!" (Ps. 137: 8-9). Here the psalm is telling us to bury sins while they are still small with the rock that is Christ, before they grow bigger. We should not wait until we fall into the sin of hatred for a person. Rather, when we start noticing that our dealings, thoughts and words with him are starting to change, we should be disciplined lest it develops deeper into something worse.

Therefore a disciplined person does not allow sin to reach its depth. He is disciplined from the beginning in order to avoid falling. The best expression in fighting against sin is when St. Paul says, "You have not yet resisted to bloodshed, striving against sin." (Heb 12:4). A disciplined person resists till bloodshed, even if it leads to martyrdom, rather than to fall into sin.

Let us be disciplined in small and large things. Let

us be weary when naming things as 'small'. The sin that destroyed the entire world was 'eating from a tree'. Someone may think that such an act is trivial. What is the problem or sin to eat from a tree? Yet the issue was greater than just eating from a tree.

The prayers of saints are really astonishing! A great saint prayed saying, 'I am the sinner, the rotten, the destroyed...' Why the use of such harsh words? It is evident that sin is not small in his sight. He is so disciplined! Sin for him is deforming the divine image on which man was created. It is not small because sin is separation from God.

To summarise, life of discipline involves two things:

1- Honesty in the spiritual life

2- Seriousness in the spiritual life

For a person to be disciplined he has to be honest and serious in his spiritual life.

SERIOUSNESS IN THE
SPIRITUAL LIFE

How can a person be serious in his spiritual life? Seriousness is a kind of maturity. It requires a balanced and strong personality. A serious person respects himself and others, and maintains good principles and values.

The difference between the saints and lay people is that the saints led a serious spiritual life. They had a serious relationship with God. They were not reluctant, complacent, or negligent. They did not falter between two opinions, nor reverse backwards.

The saints who repented found it to be a turning point in their life. Some of them include; St. Moses the Black, St. Augustine, St. Mary the Egyptian and St. Pelagia. They all repented and did not return to their sinful ways. They were serious in their repentance. This was the reason they progressed to purity and perfection.

It is the same with the monk who is serious in his spiritual and monastic life. He progresses gradually, never going back to his old life style when he was a layman. There are some monks who weep for their old sins as the saying goes, "enter into your cell and weep for your sins". It is very hurtful when a monk weeps for new sins committed. Thus the monk is not only repenting over old news but over new sins. It is evident then that this monk did not truly repent yet and he is not taking monasticism seriously.

One should be like St. Arsanius who was serious in his monastic life, examining himself daily.

Let us ask ourselves 'what have we done that is pleasing to God and what have we done to hurt Him'? The fathers who excelled in their monastic life were serious. The likes of which include; Maximus and Domadius, of which one of them was quite young, St. John the Short, St. Tadros the disciple of St. Pahkoum, St. Shenouda who achieved a high spiritual level at a young age and St. Mark the Recluse who used to fast till the ninth hour when he was just a child. All of these people were serious in their spiritual life.

There is a confronting verse for those who are

reluctant in their spiritual life, "Cursed is he who does the work of the Lord deceitfully." (Jer 48:10). All the deeds of those who followed God in holiness were serious. Abraham, the father of fathers, led an obedient life. He was so serious to the extent that when he was asked to sacrifice his only son he was obedient and faithful until the end.

A serious person is always successful and disciplined in everything, whether it is a monastic deed or another responsibility. They are serious, persistent and labour in their spiritual life, serving God with all their power and ability. They offer their will and heart, never falling short of anything. They rely on the grace granted to them, getting closer to God daily. Thus, they are always growing spiritually and improving their relationship with God as a result of living seriously in their spirituality.

There is a saying, "the path to hell is furnished with excuses and justifications." People usually excuse themselves and find justifications for sins, but a serious person faces the obstacles in their life and tries to overcome them. They never make excuses for themselves.

A serious person is not lazy but always "fervent in spirit" (Acts 18: 25) as said about St. Isaiah the Recluse.

Our teacher St. Paul the Apostle says, "Run in such a way that you may obtain it." (1 Cor. 9: 24). He did not say walk, but rather run. The person who is serious in his spiritual life is the one truly running.

A serious person exerts every effort in their spiritual life. They are not only dependant on the divine support but they work for God with all their might so there is no room for laziness. They tire for the sake of God, as it is written to the Angel of Ephesus, "I know your works, love, service, faith and your patience." (Rev 2:19). Even as the Lord said to St. Paul of Tammuh "Enough exhaustion my beloved Paul." Imagine, a person exerts so much effort that God would tell him enough?!

A serious person is honest in his relationship with God and himself. He does not accept half solutions, never compromising in his spirituality. His continuous target is perfection, "Therefore you shall be perfect, as your Father in heaven is Perfect." (Matt 5: 48).

Joseph could have justified himself because his circumstances were difficult and he was presented with various pressures from the outside, yet he was very serious in his spirituality. Thus it was said about the righteous man, "and whatever he does shall prosper." (Ps 1: 3). Why would he prosper in whatever he does? He would prosper because he is doing everything seriously in monasticism, in service, and in every responsibility laid upon him.

A serious person does not spoil himself or make excuses. He never spoils himself at the cost of his spirituality. He always works with strictness and enthusiasm, progressing quickly. He is not hesitant, trying to reach the ideal as much as he can. Those who do not live strictly in their spiritual life end up losing the seriousness of their target. They lose commitment to God when they lose seriousness.

Let us evaluate an Old Testament character: Jephthah the Gileadite. He vowed that the first thing to meet him on his way back from victory, he would offer it up as a burnt offering. It happened that his only daughter was the one who met him and because he was serious, he offered her. We do not want to judge here whether it was right or wrong, but we want to say that he was mentioned among the men of faith in Hebrews chapter 11. He carried out his vow because he was serious.

Samson lost himself and his commitment to God. Though he was mighty he was a reluctant in his vow and broke it, losing his strength and himself for a long period.

When the children of Israel departed Egypt, they

were not serious at all in their relationship with God. They often felt tired and complained, until they said, "Oh, that we had died by the hand of the Lord in the land of Egypt, when we sat by the pots of meat and when we ate bread to the full!" (Ex.16: 3). They regretted following God.

He who does not live seriously in spirituality may reach this level at a certain time and regret following God. He who is continuously struggling will never think of the past due to his fervent struggle. He is always progressing as his target is fixed. An unclear target or a hesitant one makes a person's life unsettled.

A serious person in spirituality is always active, never wasting time in arguments. A non-serious person always argues, even in each virtue or principle. He does not want to be committed to anything, just arguing instead of acting.

There are no spiritual lapses in a serious person's life. On the contrary, the one who is not serious is up and down all the time like a person building and falling. Whatever he achieved in a week would be lost by the next. His heart is dishonest with God, unstable in his principles always changing.

A serious person pushes himself at all times to fulfil

God's commandments in order to find pleasure in God. He does not care about superficial issues, but cares about the essence of spirituality. One person who was serious in his spiritual life said, "I cannot remember the devils making me fall in the same sin twice." Therefore, if he falls once he learns his lesson and never falls again in the same sin. It may be that when he fell he did not take good care, or that he fell out of ignorance, but he would not allow himself to commit the same sin twice.

Among those who were not serious in their relationship with God was Lot's wife. What a disaster! She actually left the land of Sodom but she was not serious. The angel was holding her hand, but still she was not serious. She turned into a pillar of salt while holding the angel's hand because her departure from Sodom was coming out of a dishonest heart. Ananias and Sapphira wanted to give their money to God, but they were not genuine so they only gave a portion and paid their lives as a price for not being serious.

A serious person does not falter between two opinions. He fixes his face towards Jerusalem. He never changes his worship, his spiritual practices and how he deals with people. He is always serious in his promises and vows to God.

How about the seriousness of the children of God

mentioned in the Holy Bible " We know that whoever is born of God does not sin" (1 John 5: 18), also, "and he cannot sin" (1 John 3: 9). He does not know how to sin, and the wicked one does not touch him. Why? Because he is firm like a rock, not shaken by any storms or rains.

A serious person does not look for the easy way out and does not fear the narrow gate, but faces hardships with a steadfast heart and faith.

A non-serious person might sleep and dream of paradise. He may think that grace has carried him and taken him to paradise. The serious one continually struggles to reach Paradise.

A serious person has the virtue of commitment in his life. He is committed to every word that he utters. He sticks to his principles and values, and even what he says in his prayers, such as 'forgive us our trespasses as we forgive to those who trespass against us'.

In our prayers, we say, 'as we forgive'; "I drench my couch with my tears." (Ps 6: 6), and "O God, You are my God; early will I seek You;" (Ps.63:1) but we do not fulfil these words seriously.

A person who is uncommitted always justifies his commitment with the wrong concepts of grace and freedom in Christ.

The Remembrance of Evil Entailing Death

There are two types of the remembrance of evil:

The first type is to remember one's sin in a remorseful manner, rebuking oneself about which David the Prophet said, "My sin is always before me." However, we should not consider 'My sin is always before me' without ignoring the verse "All night I make my bed swim, I drench my couch with my tears." (Ps.6:6). We should meditate on both verses together; otherwise we will enter into the other aspect of the remembrance of evil which is harmful.

The second type is when a person remembers his sin and wishes to go back and commit it again. This can lead to a person defiling his mind with that sin. This is what we call in the Holy Liturgy, "the remembrance of evil entailing death" which leads to spiritual death.

In the fraction at the end of the Liturgy we pray, "Cast away from us every displeasing thought which does not please Your goodness, O God, the Lover of mankind." We also pray, "purify our hearts, thoughts and consciences", and at the end of each prayer in the Agpia we pray, "Purify our bodies, set right our thoughts, and cleanse our intentions."

In order to distinguish between the two types of remembrance of evil, we point out that recalling the title of the sin does not necessarily harm the person, but rather remembering the sin in detail is what harms the person. A person should not remember the details of any sin especially what we call the excitable sins or the sensual sins. It is very inappropriate to think of its details; otherwise you may fall into, "the memory of evil entailing death."

Examples of remembering sins that can entail death:

Remembering emotional sins such as the sin of anger may lead to the remembrance of evil entailing death. After remembering a sin that made us angry we would then pray to God to forgive us for this sin. Yet if we keep remembering the details of this sin we will go back to being angry, and the memory of the evil will take us back to the same sin. As an example, a person might keep remembering a disagreement between himself and someone else, and after remembering the details he will go back to the original emotional feelings. It is the same with the sin of envy, the desire of possession, haughtiness, vain glory...etc.

Concerning the desire of adultery and lust, if a person keeps remembering its details it will harm him again. Therefore any person with previous sins should not remember its details or go back to it. As a general rule we say that sinful thoughts are not barren, but they produce other sinful thoughts. If you remember a sinful thought, it will bring numerous other sinful thoughts. It is better to flee from the lustful thoughts, because this kind haunts and lingers in one's mind. Do not deceive yourself by trying to engage the thought; it is better to flee it. A certain thought might last with some people for days and months, remembering it day and night. Remembering sinful thoughts is a means of going back to the old man. It is a kind of negativity, going backwards. A person should be positive with his thinking, to meditate on holy spiritual matters which lifts his mind to God, which protects him from evil thoughts. There is a phrase which we call "shy thinking". It means that if a person is always thinking of holy matters and a sinful thought hits him, he would be ashamed saying to himself, "how can I can think of such matters while my mind is busy with Divine thoughts?!" And so, he will ignore them.

As mentioned before, sinful thoughts produce more sinful thoughts. Thus we should cast away the sinful thought from the beginning by being strong in fighting against them. If you accept sinful thoughts, you will become weaker, and you will find it harder to overcome them. You therefore betray God by accepting the evil thought, and cast the grace of God out of your heart. You then become weaker and the devil enters into your heart.

If you accept a thought, it will not be alone but it will bring other thoughts as well. You may therefore become weaker and weaker, and to combat these thoughts always remember the Psalm, "Praise the LORD, O Jerusalem! Praise your God, O Zion! For He has strengthened the bars of your gates; He has blessed your children within you." (Ps. 147). If you allow accept a thought, you do not know where it could lead. Never start negotiating with thoughts which are very clearly sinful. If you start negotiating with them, then you are at risk of turning them into actions. If you negotiate with such thoughts, it means that you are not serious in your spiritual life. Do not deceive yourself by trying to resist and overcome them as you have sinful desires in your heart. If you want to be victorious cast thoughts away immediately, as one of the saints said, "even if you win you may have stained your mind throughout the way." A thought which stains your mind by any means would have authority over you and grow deeper in the form of dreams and doubts. It has been imprinted in your subconscious mind. Believe me, all the devil is after is negotiation with thoughts. Refusing to do so gives him a hard time. If you want to abase him, do not talk to him.

Eve started to negotiate with the devil, "Has God indeed said, 'You shall not eat of every tree of the garden?' Eve answered that God even said, "You shall not eat it, nor shall you touch it, lest you die." How strong was Eve in the start of the conversation but how did it end!? She accepted negotiation with the devil and in the end she ate from the forbidden tree and also pushed Adam to do so. Do not think that having a good start will necessarily remain constant. The devil starts pulling the thread, and then leaves it to you. He will keep pulling you until you fall at the end. If the war keeps going on between you and the devil, it is not in your favour. Do not try to win but escape. In escaping is victory.

The thoughts affect the heart, senses, and the body. For example, when you become angry your body temperature will rise, affecting your appearance and body language. Thoughts are like the head of a big family. It has friends and relatives. Anger will lead you to judgment, then defaming, then revenge, then justification and defending yourself. You never know where you will end up. Always close the door to harmful thoughts, remembering the verse, "A garden enclosed is my sister, my spouse, a spring shut up, a fountain sealed." (Songs 4: 12). You should be a closed garden before the enemies. Let us stay away from harmful thoughts and their origin, whether the thoughts come from your senses, by reading, by hearing, from within or from others. If you keep thinking about harmful thoughts, it means that you are still living in sin. This means that you are giving the thought a chance to grow and to develop into other thoughts. It is like Ahab who negotiated with his thoughts and ended up killing Naboth. Also at first Cain controlled his thoughts, but when he gave them a chance and negotiated with them, they overcame him. You will be defeated if you negotiate with harmful thoughts. You may scream out, "the thoughts are tiring me", but actually you are the one who is stirring the thoughts and negotiating with them.

You may ask, should I not rebuke myself for my sins? Well let it be a general rebuke concerning emotional sins. Do not go into its details. The devil usually comes hiding in thoughts. He may even camouflage the harmful thought in the form of a virtue. Take for example fasting. Would the devil tell you openly 'do not fast'? Impossible! Your answer would be 'I have to obey God more than people, even to martyrdom.' The devil is not that naive. I will tell you the devil's idea to deprive you from fasting; he will tell you how wonderful prostrations and vigils are during fasting. He will then start to attract you to pray more, with your confession father supporting you. The devil will convince you that your confession father wants you to progress in your spirituality and not the contrary. Therefore you become very exhausted because of too many prostrations. Your legs will become feeble. The devil then will convince you it is because you are eating so little. The devil's advice will be to nourish your body properly in order to be able to perform your prostrations. Eat a bigger meal to perform better in your spiritual vigil and prostrations. If you then say 'what about fasting'? He will answer you that God cares about the spiritual issues more than the body, and thus you will lose your fasting. You stop fasting not because of your leniency and negligence, but because of spiritual vigil, prostrations, and the love of God! This is why the Apostle says, "for we are not ignorant of his devices." (2 Cor. 2:11). If the devil advises you to do prostrations, your answer should be, 'you are not the one to tell me what to do. My confession father is guiding me. Thank you for your spiritual advice, I do not need it.'

Let us therefore escape harmful thoughts from the beginning and never give them a chance to develop. Keep your mind busy with positive things. Prevention is better than treatment!

It is also important to not to seek to know the latest news. For then you are the one bringing harmful thoughts, and then complain about it as a source of trouble in your mind!

Routine

It is possible that monasticism can just become a routine without life, understanding or benefit. Let us look at some examples to explore this.

The Words "I Have Sinned":

It is very easy that these words in monasticism can become a cover for any mistake just to avoid any blame so that the other person might say, "may God forgive you". There is no discussion, discipline, or fixing of any wrong attitude regarding the issue! If someone blames us, we would say, "I already said I have sinned, what else do I have to do"? It may be that the person saying 'I have sinned' does not even know in which way he has made a mistake. If he truly remembers all the mistakes he has committed, then the words 'I have sinned' would be meant seriously.

We may hurt someone's feelings, and then cover it with saying 'I have sinned'. How then can we not think deeply about what we have said or give account of our behaviour seriously? We should ask 'how did we hurt someone and how can we amend the situation inside our heart'? Instead we just stop at saying 'I have sinned.'

The words 'I have sinned' in monastic life should be understood deeply. It is to be said from the heart seriously, apologising in regret. Therefore knowing its true meaning will have a greater effect on a person.

Suppose someone got angry and uttered inappropriate words, and then said insincerely 'I have sinned'. How would the person in front of them know in which way they have sinned? However if the person said sincerely 'I have sinned because I did so and so', this will show the other person that he is really serious in saying, 'I have sinned' and it is not just a routine.

A person should know from the beginning of his monastic life how to deal humbly with others because the words 'I have sinned' mean that he has actually regretted his wrong doing and will try not do it again. If he repeats the matter it means that he did not feel his guilt, thus saying 'I have sinned' was just a routine.

Prostrations:

The word prostration (metania) means 'repentance'. Are we really offering repentance when we perform a prostration? It is an act of bowing with respect, submission, and humility. Do we have these feelings, or has the prostration only become a routine just like saying 'I have sinned'?

Monasticism may have taught a monk to do prostrations, yet he may be doing them without meaning or care. If the monks know the depth of the prostration while performing it, many changes would take place inside the heart. Thus when the laymen, who are not used to prostrations, witness it being performed with seriousness and depth they would become touched.

If a monk's life becomes just a routine he would lose much of his spirituality. His life would only be formalities.

'Absolve me, forgive me, may God absolve you, may God forgive you':

A monk may meet another monk and say, 'absolve me, forgive me' and the other replies, 'may God absolve you, may God forgive you'. They might say these sentences as a kind of greeting or courtesy. It may be a habit without entering into the depth its meaning.

Another example is the general absolutions. A person bowing his head hears the absolution without confessing his sins or regretting them. If he is serious during the prayer of the absolution about confessing his sins, then he will feel the grace given during the absolution.

In The Holy Liturgy:

Some people repeat parts of the liturgy as a routine without entering into the depth of their meaning. There is a prayer said by the deacon and many times no one listens or is affected by the prayer, as if nothing was said. After the commemoration of the saints the deacon responds saying: 'Let the readers recite the names of our holy fathers, the patriarchs who have departed'. Rarely does anybody say the names of the patriarchs, it is just a routine sentence said by the deacon. The congregation has become used to hearing parts of the Holy Liturgy without understanding or taking action. We should know the seriousness of the prayers.

Many of our prayers are turned into routine. When the priest faces the congregation saying, 'Peace be with you' and signs them with the cross, we do not know if he is truly giving peace and blessing from his heart to the congregation or if it is just a ritual action he is used to. He may say this without understanding or meaning.

People will feel the blessings gained through the signing of the cross if the priest is praying this sentence in truth and depth. I wonder when the congregation answer 'and with your spirit', is it coming from their hearts that the priest would have peace also or is it just a routine response?

There are other prayers that may have become a routine for us. There are many who pray 'Our Father Who art in heaven' without intending to follow the prayer and go deep into spirituality. It is just a matter of reciting the prayer quickly without contemplating on the words. We need to keep in mind that the more we memorise; the more susceptible we are to fall into routine. We have to pray and understand every word we say, not just reciting prayers quickly without noticing what we are saying. We say many Psalms that we have memorised but it is as if we have not prayed. St. Isaac the Syrian says, 'If you are fought with routine, say to yourself, I am not standing here before the Lord just to say words, I am standing here to pray.'

We can find a person who says just one Psalm with zeal able to cast out demons. Yet another person might recite 70 or more Psalms in the Agpia prayers but it is as if he did not even pray one of them. The Agpia prayers are so deep in spirituality, but praying it in a routine way is a mistake.

Let us think about our prayers. Do we pray with understanding and depth?

The same applies to fasting. The monk fasts all the church fasts but are they just done in a routine way?

The Holy Communion:

The monk partakes of the Holy Communion frequently. Does it become a routine?

Any person who is used to regularly partaking of Holy Communion may do so as a habit. It may be that preparing for Holy Communion is no longer an important issue. For a priest it may be his turn to pray and thus he has to partake of Holy Communion regardless if he is prepared or repentant. It is more important for him to perform the duty and think of these issues later, or not even at all.

As we have mentioned previously, the Psalms may become a routine while others pray them with true depth. Some claim that the Psalms are a canon they have to finish, ignoring the understanding, meditation, and reverence of the Psalms. They do not consider these matters often.

The Church And Its Holiness:

Attending the church may also become a routine. Those visiting the monastery feel the blessing of the church. Every aspect of the monastery becomes a blessing for them, even the dust and ground of the monastery and its surrounding walls. They put their hands on the walls of the monastery to gain blessings. They also gain the blessing of the entire wilderness, the places surrounding the monastery, and the desert land.

Let us ask ourselves, has entering these holy places become a routine for us? Have we lost the spirituality, awe, and respect? Let us be weary lest our spiritual life become a routine and worship a habit. Prayer should not be just readings and tunes. A person living in this routine would find himself just practising the formality of the life of worship, while ignoring the inner depth. He may live for a long time in this spiritual life but as someone who has not even started!

We need to be serious in our spiritual life, to understand and practise what we are doing. We also need to perform everything from the depth of our hearts. It is a matter of honesty with ourselves and discovering the meanings of our practices.

Service:

Here we do not mean the service outside the monastery, but inside. If someone is delegated a service, is he serving a person or a specific area in the monastery? Sometimes service becomes an authority. The core of service for a person may be turned into a field of authority and power. A person can become haughty, loud, commanding and rebuking. They may reject other people's opinion simply because of their authority. Thus, the word 'service' loses its meaning.

The same happens outside the monastery. Some might say that they are a servant at a particular church, while they are actually appointing themselves as the manager of the church. Therefore the word service has become a routine and lost its spirituality. When appointed a responsibility in the monastery, do I feel that I am a servant in this responsibility? A servant is truly one who serves the needs of the monastery and others.

I wish that every priest while washing his hands in the Liturgy saying, "I wash my hands in purity", would actually mean that he is purifying himself in order to stand pure before God in this service. It is not just a matter of washing hands as a rite without spirituality.

These are just some examples of routine yet there are so many details related to this topic. We have to review our spiritual life in order to be accepted before God.

The Inner Work

The Lord always cares about the inside, not the outside – our fathers call it "the inner person". The Lord says, "My son, give me your heart." (Prov 23:26). He truly cares about the work inside a person, rather than the outside. The Lord knows those who outwardly worship while their heart is void of the love of God. He spoke of them saying, "This people honours Me with their lips, but their heart is far from Me." (Mark 7:6).

In the book of Isaiah God refused outer worship. He refused incense that was offered without true prayer saying; "Incense is an abomination to Me" (Is 1:13). He also refused sacrifices, burnt offerings, feasts and celebrations that were only outwardly. He mentioned prayers that were void of the love of God saying, "When you spread out your hands, I will hide My eyes from you; even though you make many prayers, I will not hear. Your hands are full of blood." (Is 1:15). He desires worship with a heart filled with the love of God.

How beautiful is the verse, "The royal daughter is all glorious within the palace... her clothing is woven with gold. She shall be brought to the King in robes of many colours." (Ps 45:13-14). The royal daughter's glory lies within her. God is more concerned about what is inside the heart rather than the outside.

The Lord harshly criticised the scribes and Pharisees for their hypocrisy saying, "Woe to you, scribes and Pharisees, hypocrites! For you are like whitewashed tombs which indeed appear beautiful outwardly, but inside are full of dead men's bones and all uncleanness. Even so you also outwardly appear righteous to men, but inside you are full of hypocrisy and lawlessness." (Matt. 23: 27-28). They appeared righteous on the outside but on the inside they were empty. He also spoke about them saying that they cleanse the outside of the cup and dish, but on the inside they are full of extortion and self-indulgence. He cursed the fig tree because it had plenty of leaves but bore no fruit. The tree had a beautiful outer appearance but was empty inside. God seeks inner work. He cares about what is inside our heart, not how we look on the outside.

Even if a person appears to be doing nothing on the outside, he may be performing inner work which is far more important. Such a person can be likened to a seed that is full of life yet appears dead. As soon as the seed is sowed and irrigated, roots grow deep into the earth and a stem grows above the surface.

Another good example of inner work is the silk worm. When it is in the cocoon it does not move and looks completely dead, however there are things happening inside. After a period of stillness, a beautiful butterfly comes out. This shows that there was inner work, that no one knew about, which brought forth fruits.

The Apostle said, "be transformed by the renewing of your mind." (Rom 12:2). That is, re-direct your thoughts and appreciate different things that the inner work of your mind may be renewed.

Types of Inner Work:

1. Inner work with God – inner work between yourself and God. For example, struggling with God to receive strength to work on your inner life.

2. Inner work with oneself – a decision concerning what you should do.

3. The inner work of the devil – this is an inner work you are fighting against. You have to subdue all your thoughts to Christ and obey Him as St Paul says, "bringing every thought into captivity of the obedience of Christ."(2 Cor 10:5).

4. The inner work of desires, cravings, thoughts and decisions.

Many monks and hermits like the inner wilderness. I strongly believe that the inner wilderness is inside us, rather than just the physical location.

Imagine a monk living in a cave in the inner wilderness and his thoughts are occupied with the affairs of the monastery or the world. Is he living in the inner wilderness? The inner wilderness is within our heart. It is an untrodden ground without water.

The fathers always advised the monks to focus on their inner work. Many even decided to live in solitude up on the mountains for the sake of their inner work.

Let us know distinguish between inner and outer work in the spiritual life:

Prayer:

Outer work involves praying the psalms, completing one's canon and saying personal prayers, yet all of these are in vain unless they are accompanied by the inner work of a relationship with God. You need to feel as though you are talking to God, not just repeating words. There should be love, reverence, humility and warmth – all of these are the inner work of a "fervent spirit." (Rom 12:11). We need to understand and meditate upon every word we say. To just read a psalm and quickly move onto the next is just an outward practice.

Those who make one prostration after another, what do your prostrations mean? When you bend your knees and bow your head, do you forget to submit your soul? When you make a prostration before the altar, do you humble yourself before God or do you approach Him with haughtiness and a proud heart? The psalm says, "My soul clings to the dust" (Ps 119:25), not "my head clings to the dust".

In "The Paradise of the Fathers" one of the monks told his father that he made a prostration but his brother did not accept it. His father replied saying that his prostration was not valid because it was offered with a heart full of pride.

When we pray, we often claim to do things that we actually do not. For example we say "Rejoice at [God's] word as one who finds great treasure" (Ps 119:162); when in reality we are just repeating words. We also say, "[we] will lift up [our] hands in Your name. [Our] soul[s] shall be satisfied as with marrow and fatness..." (Ps 63: 4-5). Raising our hands is an outer work, while our soul becoming satisfied is an inner work. Where do you stand amidst this? Do you just "lift up your hands" or do you achieve the inner work of "my soul shall be satisfied"?

Fasting:

On the outside, fasting is abstaining from food or eating vegetarian food. However the inner aspect of fasting surpasses materialistic things. It involves subduing the body, overcoming the ego and not satisfying the desires of the flesh. When you fast, are you engaged with the outer work or the inner work? I am worried that people are merely concerned with the external aspects of fasting, not the inner.

A spiritual father once told a monk who was merely concerned with outer works, "Do not comfort yourself, my brother, because you are wearing black." A black garment merely forms an external appearance. We need to look inside our hearts. There should be inner work. Have we died to the world? Have you renounced everything in the world, or do you still enjoy having possessions? Dying to the world involves renouncing everything related to the world. "Do not love the world or the things in the world… for the world is passing away, and the lust of it."

Reading:

Outer work is reading, while inner work is understanding and meditating. Yet even these are considered shallow. Inner work is deeper. It involves living the words you have read such that it becomes a doctrine. The word has power from the Holy Spirit to help you. Do you have the power of the Holy Spirit dwelling inside you? For example, St Anthony heard a verse that moved his heart and completely changed his life. He performed inner work.

Confession:

The outer work is confessing one's sins, while the inner work is a strong sense of regret and remorse. It involves being truly repentant and making a decision not to commit the same sins again. That is why the sacrament of confession is often called the "the Mystery of Repentance". It requires one to hate sin. All these things are required for confession. However if one is merely confessing his sins without sincere repentance, it is in vain. Confession is not just a verbal revelation of one's sins; there is also an inner work.

When the prodigal son returned to his father he said, "I have sinned against heaven and before you." (Luke 15:18). However, before he returned to his father he came back to himself and thought about how miserable he was. He consequently decided to change his life. These are all inner works prior and accompanying to confession.

Silence:

Outer work involves the absence of speaking, while inner work involves quieting one's senses, thoughts and heart. One may not speak or verbally criticise others, but on the inside they are constantly criticising those around them. How can we say that such a person is living in silence? Sometimes our minds and hearts speak more than our tongues. God desires continuous inner work.

Chastity:

In regards to chastity outer work involves refraining from physical sin, while inner work involves hating the sin with all our heart. One of the fathers said, "Many have chaste bodies but they are adulterers inside."

One may have a chaste body but inside is full of evil thoughts and desires.

Repentance involves replacing one desire with another. That is, replacing the worldly desires with those concerning God and His Heavenly Kingdom. Repentance involves directing the desires of the heart to God. It is not about merely abstaining from sin but also to hate sin. True repentance is due to the love of God and the desire for spirituality.

He who is concerned about the inner work in his heart is close to God. His spirituality will be hidden inside. However, the Father who sees in secret rewards openly.

A person may give alms but is full of hatred inside, or he may give to show off. We call charity a deed of mercy and giving. The inner work is mercy, while the outer work is giving.

A Life of Struggle

Monasticism is a life of struggle. When a person decides to pursue a virtuous life, the devil starts to envy him. However for the person who is reluctant in his spiritual life the devils do not necessarily need to attack him as he is already living defeated.

The devils strongly war against the elders and those struggling in the life of monasticism. A young monk once approached St. Bishoy and said, "Please pray for me, the devils are strongly attacking me." When St. Bishoy started to pray for him, the devil appeared to him and said, "I never knew that this brother was a monk. Who is he that I may fight him?"

A "working monk" is one who is engaged in spiritual work. Such work may involve completing his canon, staying away from the desires of the world and preserving his senses. These are all considered inner wars. A monk who has not yet started to "work" may not face these wars, or he might face wars similar to those experienced by laymen.

When St. Paul lived with St. Anthony he wanted to be with him all the time as he sought refuge in his prayers. However, St. Anthony told him to depart and live in his own cell. Although St. Paul begged St. Anthony to stay with him, he insisted that he return to his cell so that he may fight the devils.

How To Overcome The Wars of The Devil:

Those who read about the demonic wars our fathers experienced will notice very strange things. The greatest weapons for fighting devils are humility, confession and prayer.

1. Humility brings grace to save a person.

2. Confession discloses the work of the devil and enables a person to obtain advice from their spiritual father.

3. Prayer gives a person power from God.

It is very rare for a devil to overcome a person who arms himself with these weapons.

Fighting the devils needs wisdom, experience and discernment. The Bible tells us to "test the spirits." (1 John 4:1). Man needs to discern where his thoughts are coming from – are they from God, the devil or another source? St. Paul the Apostle said, "we are not ignorant of his devices" (2 Cor 2:11) and "those who by reason of use have their senses exercised to discern both good and evil" (Heb 5:14). "Exercise" your spiritual senses so that you may know the wars of the devils.

St Oghris was one of the fathers who spoke a lot about demonic warfare and how to overcome the devils. He used to fight every evil thought with a biblical verse. He used to say: "If this particular thought comes to your mind, recite this verse…"

The Wars of The Devil:

An experienced monk is not necessarily one who is old in age or has spent many years in monasticism. Rather he is a monk who has fought the devil, knows his tricks and thoughts, and how to overcome them. St. Anthony said, "I saw the traps of the devils spread over the whole earth."

The devil is very patient. It is written in "The Paradise

of the Fathers" that the devil fought a monk for 50 years in an attempt to make him fall into a particular sin. The devil never gets bored or gives up. He can spend a long period of time focusing on one particular sin, gradually implementing his traps in an attempt to make one fall. Another example is seen when the devil made Jacob fall. The devil used many steps, each building up from the previous to make him fall. Some of the attacks of the devils cause people to immediately fall, whereas others take years to cause one to stumble. The devil is very patient; the most important thing for him is that he achieves a result in the end.

The devil is also very cunning and intelligent. It is written that, "The serpent was more cunning than any beast of the field." (Gen 3:1). He is very knowledgeable. St Isaac said, "you are fighting someone with 7000 years of experience in fighting humans... he has deeply studied human nature. He knows all its weakness, and the ways to entice a person to make him fall." He can attack from the left and right depending on the situation and the person he is fighting.

If you ask me who the greatest psychologist in the world is, I would answer the devil. He has the most experience. He has tested thousands of souls and many different types of personalities. He knows who will work with him and who will reject him. Though he may attack an individual for several years, he never gives up or regards such a person as unworthwhile. The devil attacks everyone. We are all vulnerable to fall. "There is none righteous, no, not one... they have all turned aside; they have together become unprofitable; there is none who does good, no, not one." (Rom 3:12). This verse probably makes the devil rejoice.

The devil knows the Bible. He memorises it and uses its verses to deceive people. He even used bible verses with misleading interpretations to tempt Jesus.

The devil has many talents. He knows all about music, poetry, philosophy, painting, sculpture...etc. He knows all the different forms of amusements and attempts to make the monk co-operate with him. The devil makes promises but does not keep them. "He is a liar and the father of it." (John 8:44).

If the devil wants someone to fall into a particular sin, he does not immediately fight him with that sin. Instead, he first tries to encourage them to abandon reading of the Bible, praying the psalms, meditations, and meeting with their confession father. He paves the way for a person to become reluctant in his spiritual life and live for himself. He carefully plans how he will start the war; it is not a random attack.

The devil often encourages people to fall into sins that will eventually lead to the original sin he was planning to achieve. For example, if the devil wanted to fight someone with adultery, he would first start with other sins such as laziness, gluttony, and materialism. Then when he comes to tempt the person with the sin of adultery, he finds that they are more susceptible to commit it. That way he may attack suddenly and the person will lose control of everything.

The devil can also appear in the form of an angel or a saint. He can say wonderful spiritual words, and introduce sin as a virtue. The Lord said, "beware of false prophets, who come to you in sheep's clothing, but inwardly they are ravenous wolves." (Matt 7:15). That is, the devil clothes sin in sheep's clothing such that it may appear to be a virtue.

Say for example that the devil wanted a monk to leave his monastery and return to the world; do you know what he would do? He would first make him increase his prayers, prostrations, seclusion and asceticism. Then he will make him confront his confession father who will tell him that he is going to the extreme. The monk will then start to doubt his confession father, which is a well-known demonic war, and consequently leave his confession father. He will then continue his extreme ascetic practices and eventually fall into the sin of pride.

The next step involves him having visions, false dreams and conversations that will pull him down. Then amidst all these situations the devil will tempt the monk to fall into sin.

The devil often suggests an idea to a person and insists that he performs it quickly. He does this so that a person does not have the chance to pray or seek the advice of his confession father. St Isaac said, "If a thought enters your mind and insists that it must be carried out quickly, know that it is from the devil." God likes all issues to be dealt with in a calm manner.

The devil starts by attacking gradually. He makes things appear different to what they are in reality. He does not become ashamed when he is exposed, but rather tries to cover up one sin with another. He leads people into an endless chain of sins. He is never satisfied just when a person falls, he always wants more. He keeps fighting until the person totally despairs over his salvation and consequently becomes a toy in the devil's hands. David refers to such despair when he says, "Many are they who say of me, 'There is no help for him in God.'" (Ps 3:2). The devil tries to turn sin into a habit, such that a person sins without even thinking about it or finding any pleasure in doing it.

Just as the devil recruited an army of fallen angels,

he also seeks to recruit an army of people. He wants an army to help him make others fall. The devil can possess people and make them a member of his kingdom. Those who are demon possessed speak words in a voice that is not their own. They possess the knowledge and have the thoughts of the devil inhabiting them. The person becomes the devil's slave. This is a very difficult situation.

In the stories of the saints we find many examples when the devil deceived great saints. For example, the devil tricked St. Ghalion into quickly escaping to the wilderness to become a hermit without even consulting his spiritual father. Ghalion lived in solitude in the monastery for approximately 60 years, until he was advanced in age. The devil caused several other hermits to fall. For example, St Timothy the hermit fell while he was living in solitude. St Jacob the Recluse also fell while he was living in solitude and performing miracles. David the Psalmist fell when he was a prophet and the anointed of the Lord. The devil does not fear anyone. We might think that he spares the hermits and prophets, but he does not.

The devil even dared to tempt Christ after His baptism when he heard a voice from heaven say: "This is My Beloved Son" (Matt 3:17).

Never think for a moment that you cannot be tempted by the devil. Thus we need to always live in the fear of God and conduct ourselves with discipline. The bible says "Conduct yourselves throughout the time of your stay here in fear" (1 Peter 1:17). "Work out your own salvation with fear and trembling" (Phil 2:12). "Therefore let him who thinks he stands take heed lest he fall" (1 Cor 10:12).

Therefore, we always need to pray to God and ask Him to sanctify us. Let us ask Him to "Purge [us] with hyssop, and [we] shall be clean" (Ps 51:7).

TIME FOR A MONK

Here we will draw upon the issue of time for a monk and how he can use it efficiently. Time can be used beneficially or harmfully. How a monk uses his time is the difference between the most holy and a reluctant monk. Is time working with or against him? Our aim is to use time for spiritual work. The more time used for spiritual work, the deeper our relationship with God will be and the more clear and developed our monastic life will be.

The question is 'how do I make use of time'? Some might say "I am too busy!" Let us mention a few points here:

Be comfortable performing spiritual work during the night. Those who are comfortable performing spiritual work at night will reap in the morning, especially in the longer nights of winter. We can make use of the night for spiritual work as the Psalmist says, "by night stand in the house of the Lord, lift up your hands in the sanctuary, and bless the Lord." (Ps 134:1) St. Isaac the Syrian used to say 'the night is specified for prayer". St. Arsanius used to spend the whole night in prayer. He looked to the east with the sun behind him, and waited till the sun came in front of him. It was said about our Lord Jesus Christ that He used to spend the whole night in prayer.

At night there are no meetings. There are no people to talk with or any sort of interruptions. Try to make efficient use of the night. When we have light we can spend time reading or writing, but when there is no light we can spend time for prayers, psalms, meditations, self-reflection, talking to God, and singing hymns and praises. All of these can be performed at night. This is the first remark.

It is also a good idea to have an organised schedule for the night. Those who do not have a schedule can become confused.

It is good to train ourselves to practise spiritual work during physical work. This can be like a secret prayer during work and it is easily possible. Let us train ourselves to pray while walking, working, and being with people. Thus our hearts will always be busy with God in continuous short prayers, especially from the memorisation of the Psalms.

We must give to God the first fruits of our time, as much as possible, in order to give Him the best. He is the first Person we should talk to during the day and we should not be busy with anyone else. If it so happens that we do not have much time for God, then we have to make time at a minimum. It is a good idea to rest during the day for an hour or two as this will help us stay awake during the night. Those who spend the whole day working will feel tired at night.

We should always remember that originally time is authored by God, not by us. When we have consecrated our life to God, all our time becomes God's. We cannot convince ourselves of the contrary. All our time is truly authored by God.

Let me tell you, your time is your life. If we lose our time then we are losing our life! Therefore our time should be used for spiritual growth. The more time that has passed, the greater our building of spirituality should be. Ask yourself 'how high is that spiritual building'?

There are saints who greatly progressed spiritually in a very short time because they used their time seriously. They were elevated to the level of spiritual leadership while still being young, such as Saint Tadros the disciple of St. Pakhomius, and St. John the Short about whom it was said; "The entire Scetis was hanged on his finger." They were both spiritual leaders of their monasteries while still at young ages.

Among those youth who excelled in the monastic life was St. Misael the Hermit. At just 18 years of age he became a hermit after spending around four years in the monastery. He took his spiritual life seriously and made use of every minute of his time.

Also among the youth who progressed quickly in the spiritual life were St. Maximus and St. Domadius. They made proper use of their time and never let a single moment pass without a spiritual deed. Truly, constant spiritual deeds bear fruits.

Disruptions to our spiritual life:

Work: The solution for work disrupting our spiritual life is night time prayer and prayer during work. If we succeed in this spiritual work, the Abbot may help us in relieving us from some of the responsibilities to gain more time for spiritual growth. The reverse is also true.

The Abbot cannot give more time for a monk who is aimless and talking all day, otherwise he will just have more time to talk and waste his time. However if a monk is successful in his spiritual work, the monastery will give him more time and will benefit from it.

Familiarity & friendships: The risk that friendships could disrupt our spiritual life occurs when too much conversation in non-beneficial and harmful issues are discussed. Rarely when two people sit together do they build up each other or talk about something spiritually useful. While sitting with our friends let us try to talk about spiritual issues.

Sleeping: Sleeping may disrupt a monk's spiritual life. For example, a monk may remain idle in his cell for a long time so that he falls asleep for extended periods. The dangerous thing is that over-sleeping could result in harmful thoughts. A person should be wise and know the exact needs of his body. Does he need some sleep or is it just a case of being lazy and slothful?

Thoughts: Thoughts can disrupt a monk's spiritual life. This is especially true to those who follow their own desires in any issue, even if it is trivial or non-spiritual. The enemy of goodness will make the most trivial matters look great and important so that a monk would constantly think about them. Sometimes you can find a monk in his cell not working, and confused how to spend his time. He keeps thinking on and on wasting his time. A person needs to control his thoughts and know how to make use of his time in a useful manner. Of course if he is not utilising his time, he is at a greater risk of being attacked by harmful thoughts.

There are some who become occupied in their cell with many trivial matters just wasting their time. They may be wasting their time in organising their cell, cooking, making tea, or talking to other people. Sometimes they remember these things as soon as the time for spiritual work is required, thus finding many distracting things to care about in the cell.

Remembrance of events: Remembering certain events can also disrupt a monk's spiritual life. Remembering events can become like movies. Every conversation, every speech, each deed, scenes and meetings may lead to reaching all sorts of harmful conclusions. Such issues might take a long time and have a deep effect. It is the same idea in following the news and being keen for updates.

There may be other personal disrupters for each monk, but the advice is that a person has to make use of his time wisely as much as possible. He has to have a spiritual work inside and outside his cell. Both works should be fixed and well organised. There should be a commitment to follow spiritual principles in the life of a monk and he has to respect his monastic time. Indeed, if a person knows how to make use of his time, the result will be two important things:

The first is remaining in the cell and scarcely leaving it as he is experiencing God.

The second is silence and tranquillity when he meets others as he is busy with his inner work. This will minimise his chance for talking and chatting.

The opposite is true if a monk does not know how to make use of his time. If a person is not doing anything productive he will quickly get out of his cell, meet other people and look for someone to chat to. He will also keep talking and talking.

Let us then always keep our heart and mind busy with God. Let us occupy our tongue in continuous prayer. Let us feel the importance of time in our life.

Spiritual Works To Make Use of Time:

Prayer: There are different types of prayers which can be divided into Psalms and church prayers. Also there are private prayers from the heart where we offer our pleadings and meditations to God. Some monks memorise the prayers of the prophets and saints from the Holy Bible or from prayer books.

Meditation in prayer takes a long time. There are some who pray quickly and do not feel that they are praying, or do not feel a connection between themselves and God. To them it is just performing a duty. Let us pray with our spirit slowly, patiently, in understanding, and with meditations.

Mix your prayers with your feelings and spirit. This of course takes time, and you will find that your time spent in prayer has doubled. Train yourself always to resist wasting time. Sit quietly with yourself and discover what is wasting your time and try to resist it.

In addition to meditation, praising and singing imprints a great affection on the soul.

Reading: Read the Holy Bible, biographies of saints, spiritual and ascetic books, and whatever you enjoy reading. Appropriate reading helps widen our religious knowledge.

Meditation: Meditation is a beneficial way to spend our time. Whether it is on a verse of the Bible, on the lives of the saints, on the characteristics of God or any other spiritual matter.

Prostrations: Prostrations are beneficially and should be accompanied with a prayer. It is important that the prostrations are more concentrated on prayer rather than the quantity. It is also a good idea that prostrations be counted on a rosary to help a person focus on prayer, rather than counting mechanically.

Writing: Translating or scribing is also beneficial.

If our time is limited then we try to experience depth in our spiritual work. Little time with depth is far better than much superficial time. The thief had the promise of salvation with one word, and the tax collector also attained salvation with one sentence. Some people have limited time, but they benefit spiritually as they have depth in all their spiritual work.

ASCETICISM IN MONASTICISM

Monasticism is a life of asceticism where one dies to the world. Asceticism leads to a life of voluntary poverty from everything.

St. Anthony obeyed the Gospel's command that says, "sell whatever you have and give to the poor." (Mark 10:21). Our monasticism is based on this principle. How can we have possessions when the Bible says "sell whatever you have"? I am going to stress on this verse. Possessions suggest that a monk is moving in a negative direction and leaving his monastic vows of obedience, chastity and voluntary poverty.

There is a higher level than just poverty, that is to be in need. A monk may be poor but still possess everything he needs, whereas our saintly fathers lived in poverty in which they were in need. The book 'the

Paradise of the Fathers' speaks a lot about possessions and the love of material things.

It is said that St. Pigimi the Hermit never owned anything in his cell, not even a cup! He used to eat from the grass and drink the dew on leaves. Similar things are said about St Moses the Hermit.

Let every monk count the utensils and pieces of furniture in his cell and then ask himself, "Am I really living in poverty?"

People often ask: "who will gain the inheritance of a monk?" The answer is the monastery. But does a monk have anything to be inherited in the first place? I do not think possessions or luxuries are appropriate in a life of monasticism. A monk may keep the essentials he needs, but not luxuries. However, needs and wants can be subjective. What may be considered a need for one person may be considered a luxury for another.

A true monk has very few needs, such as even electricity. There used to be no electricity in the monasteries. When I lived in solitude I had no electricity, even as a bishop and pope. Now there is electricity everywhere. I remained without electricity until 1977, and then they renovated my cell and added electricity.

Is electricity a need or luxury? The answer is subjective. We should examine everything very carefully. Electricity is good because it allows a monk to stay awake and read. Before there was electricity, monks used to spend the night in prayers and meditations, which are more powerful than reading and writing, because they could not use kerosene lanterns to read at night. With the introduction of electricity, our prayers have decreased in quality and quantity, as the mind is busy with the light. A monk may even spend the night with friends, talking and gossiping about others, or interfering with politics. In such cases, electricity can be troublesome for a monk.

Electricity has brought new innovations to a monk. For example, with electricity a monk may bring a cassette recorder into his cell. Also now we grab our drinks from the fridge because we have electricity, whereas we used to drink from a tap. A monk may have several things in his fridge. Where is this life of dispossession? Monasticism is a life of asceticism and deprivation, not luxury.

Monks should not have any luxuries in their cells. Our fathers used to live in caves and hollows in the mountains, and sleep on the floor. It was considered a luxury to sleep on a mat and an even greater luxury to have a blanket.

Remember, you vowed poverty on the day of your consecration. The funeral prayers are not just rituals. A monk must die to the world.

The Monk And Poverty:

Does poverty merely concern wages and money? When I was living as a monk in the monastery we never used to receive wages. A certain monk was responsible for spending money to supply the needs of the monastery, while the rest of us owned no money. I never touched money from the day I entered the monastery until I became a bishop.

How could a monk have money in his pocket? Why do monks collect money from people? Why do monks befriend laymen and accept their gifts?

What about those monks who indirectly ask visitors for gifts? For example, a monk may ask a guest for the time. If the guest asks if he would like a watch he would reply saying "no" while he may actually desire a watch and wants to say "yes".

The monks who are told to go to the city, where do they go? Do they still abide by the rules of monasticism or do they abandon their ascetic life and engage in other worldly issues?

In "The Paradise of the Fathers" it is said that a monk should wear a garment that if it is thrown outside his cell, no one would even look at it. I wonder about the state of our garments these days.

A monk may first start to think about how he can add more compartments to his cell, and before you know it he is thinking about adding another storey and a garden. What is happening here? A monk should feel as though he is in need of nothing. If he is ever asked about his needs, he should think deep within himself to realise that he needs nothing from this world. Know that if a monk starts feeling in need of something, he is starting to re-enter the world.

In the past, monks used to heal sick people through their prayers. If a monk fell sick, he used to cry out "O Lord" and ask God for healing. Many monks were healed through prayer, while others accepted their illness and patiently endured the pain. These days, we tend to yell out "Doctor! Pharmacy!" as soon as we get sick. I am not saying that a monk should only pray and not go to a doctor. I am just showing you how things have changed over the years.

The Monk And Fasting:

Monks used to fast for days, without any food or drink. There is another well-known story in "The Paradise of the Fathers" about a time in which a monk was once sent to inform his brothers about the beginning of the lent. A certain monk replied, "Which Lent are we starting? I have spent the past thirty years without knowing the beginning or end of lent. All the days of my life are the same."

We tend to care so much about Saturdays, Sundays and the Joyous Fifty Days. What about asceticism? I am sure you are much better than others, but we have to aim for a life of perfection.

Let every monk ask himself, "What are the things that I can live without? What can I remove from my cell?"

The Monk And Attire:

Some monks wear dirty clothes and walk with bare feet thinking they are practising asceticism. When they see me they say, "I have sinned, absolve me your holiness"… but this is unacceptable. We have to wear decent garments and socks so that we do not enter into trials. It is neither good to walk with bare feet or wear luxurious clothes. We should be moderate, not going to either extreme.

Some monks wear decent clothes when they are meeting visitors and do not care about their appearance inside their cells. Other monks do not care about visitors because they are only living to please God. Moderation is the best. Wear simple clothes without attracting attention to extreme asceticism.

One may say, "The monastic rules says that a monk should have no possessions and nothing has possession over him" Yet you have possessions because possessions take control over you. What I mean is that a monk cannot have many things and claim that it does not control him in some way. If having possessions did not affect him, then why is he collecting and keeping so many things in his cell? A monk has authority over the desires in his heart, otherwise he would have left his possessions and they would have no place in his heart.

A monk may claim that he possesses something but is not attached to it. If he is not attached to it, let him try to give it up. Only then will he discover whether or not he is really attached to it. For example, a layman may claim that he smokes but that it does not have authority over him. I tell him to quit but if he can't stop he is attached to smoking. Likewise, if you own something and think that you are not attached to it, leave it and see whether or not you feel anxious or suffer a sense of loss.

Compare your cell to the old cells our early fathers used to live in. Also compare the way food was prepared and eaten by our early fathers. Only then will you be able to determine whether or not you are truly living in asceticism. That is why I ask monks who want to live in solitude to live very simply, such as sitting on the floor and not having electricity. A monk must associate solitude with asceticism, serenity and having no possessions. I have never read a monastic book or heard of a father who lived in solitude and enjoyed the luxuries of this world. Let every monk deeply examine himself.

St Macarius said, "My brother, judge yourself before others judge you." There is no limit to worldly desires. Only God knows how one worldly desire can grow and lead to another desire, until a monk is overcome by these desires and loses his monasticism.

QUIETNESS IN MONASTICISM

I want to talk to you about silence, one of the virtues a monk should have. I hope to discuss how silence in monasticism can lead to peace in one's heart and life.

Monasticism is a life of silence. St. Isaac talks a lot about calming our senses so that they do not wander everywhere and collect new thoughts and images. One cannot live a life of monasticism with a disturbed mind and active senses.

There are two types of silence in monasticism – inner and outer silence.

A Silent Heart:

A monk should not be disturbed by his desires, his emotions and urge to fight back. A monk's heart should be calm just like the seashore. It should not be troubled by the noise and chaos in the world, even if a mountain was to move from its place. This is a very important and distinguishing characteristic of a monk.

A monk with a quiet heart has calm nerves. Such a monk is not easily agitated, and does not fight or yell. It was said of the Lord Jesus that, "He will not quarrel nor cry out, nor will anyone hear His voice in the streets. A bruised reed He will not break, and smoking flax He will not quench, till He sends forth justice to victory." (Matt 12:19-20). The Lord was filled with peace, His nerves were calm. Without such calmness, one's heart and soul becomes disturbed. This is inappropriate in the life of monasticism.

In the world, people may be excused if they lose their inner peace due to difficult circumstances, constant changes and the disturbing news surrounding them. Various changes and issues affect them every day. They may be suffering from problems at work, family problems, and economic or social issues. But what is a monk's excuse to lose his calmness?

Believe me; all the issues that disturb a monk are trivial. If a monk was to sit with himself and think about them deeply, he would realise that they are not worth worrying about.

A spiritual person does not pay much attention to the issues that disturb others. The devil often tries to magnify problems to annoy a monk, but a spiritual person is not affected by this. If he has died to the world, why should he be concerned about its problems? Worry is the product of desires disturbing the heart. It is inner desires, not external issues, that destroy a monk.

People worry when their heart is negatively affected by their desires. If a person does not get what he wants, he becomes disturbed. Those who have died to the world and all its desires live in peace and tranquillity.

Believe me, there are many righteous people in the world who forsake all material desires. St. Paul said, "and those who use this world as not misusing it. For the form of this world is passing away." (1 Cor 7:31). St Paul was celibate, not a monk. Monasticism did not even exist during his time, yet he spoke about the harm of loving the world. Such is also the case with St. John the Beloved who said, "Do not love the world or the things in the world. If anyone loves the world, the love of the Father is not in him. For all that is in the world – the lust of the flesh, the lust of the eyes and the pride of life – is not of the Father but is of the world. And the world is passing away, and the lust of it; but he who does the will of God abides forever." (1 John 2:15-17).

If you ever find yourself feeling disturbed, look inside your heart. There might be a desire causing you trouble. Some people may not be disturbed by desires, but by personal dignity. Something might have touched their pride. However, a monk who lives in humility does not care about such issues. His dignity comes from being in the image and presence of God. His dignity depends on inner purity that makes him worthy to unite with the Holy Spirit and the inheritance of the saints.

The saintly fathers were never worried or disturbed. They never lost their peace, even if they were tempted by the devil. There was once a monk who was annoyed by the attitudes of his brothers in the monastery. Consequently, he asked his spiritual father if he could live in solitude. His father replied, "My son, if you cannot tolerate the attitude of your brothers in the monastery, how could you fight the devils who annoy those who live in solitude?" This shows that everyone needs to train himself to remain calm, even in the face of tribulations and problems.

Every tribulation can be associated with a certain virtue. That is, God allows every temptation to be an opportunity to acquire a particular virtue. If you do not endure the temptation, you will not attain the virtue associated with it.

St. Paul, the father of hermits, said: "He who escapes from temptation escapes from God." This is because virtues follow temptations.

The person, whose heart is void of worldly desires and vainglory will not lose his peace. Nothing can disturb a person who is filled with inner peace.

David the Prophet was just a layman living in the world. He was not a monk but a man married to many women, yet he said, "Though an army may encamp against me, my heart shall not fear; though war may rise against me, in this I will be confident" (Ps 27:3). Why? His peace came from within; it was not determined by his external circumstances.

I want you to remember the following, "Let your peace come from inside your heart, not outside. If your peace was to depend on your external circumstances, it will not be long until you start to feel disturbed again. External circumstances can control you – they can make you calm one moment and worried the next."

Our peace comes from a heart that is void of all worldly desires. A heart in which the Spirit of God abides and yields forth the fruit of the Spirit.

If you are calm, everyone around you will be calm and vice versa. If you are angry, anger can cause a simple word to develop into a storm.

St. Paul the Apostle admonished the Corinthians saying, "O Corinthians! We have spoken openly to you, our heart is wide open. You are not restricted by us, but you are restricted by your own affections. Now in return for the same (I speak as to children), you also be open." (2 Cor 6:11-13). What does St. Paul mean by "open"? If one was to throw some mud in a cup of water, it will become cloudy. However, if one was to throw mud in the ocean it will not will be affected because the ocean is vast and open. Are you like the open ocean or not? Why may one word annoy a person but not another? This is because their hearts are different. A calm heart leads to calm nerves and hence calm voice, words and tone.

Calmness:

Calm people speak with a gentle voice. They neither quarrel nor cry out in the streets. Other people have loud voices and are rowdy. We often feel uneasy listening to such people as we can sense anger or tension in their voice.

Again, some people speak politely and with gentle words. Others fire aggressive or hurtful words like rocks out of their mouth. Which category do you fit in?

When the Lord spoke to the Samaritan woman, He said to her, "You have well said, 'I have no husband, for you have had five husbands, and the one whom you now have is not your husband; in that you spoke truly." (John 4:17-18). As I said before, those men were not her husbands; otherwise it wouldn't have been a sin. Nevertheless, the Lord spoke to her in a calm and gentle manner. She was touched by His gentleness and therefore replied, "Sir, I perceive that You are a prophet" (John 4:9) and later started preaching about Him.

I would advise everyone to be slow to speak and carefully choose his words before talking. People often say harsh things when they rush into speaking, without giving themselves time to think about what they are going to say. A spiritual person listens to St. James who said, "let every man be swift to hear, slow to speak, slow to wrath; for the wrath of man does not produce the righteousness of God." (James 1:19-20).

I wish that everyone would examine his words, are they gentle or hurtful?

Calmness of the features and gestures accompanies calmness of the nerves and speech. A spiritual person has calm features. Peace is seen in his face which appears like that of an angel, unlike those who are angry or rebellious.

We tend to enjoy being with people who have calm features as they make us feel comfortable. St Athanasius once said, "It is enough for those who are bitter or disturbed to look at St Anthony's face to be filled with peace." St Anthony was overflowing with peace!

People living in the world often obtain peace when they look at monks and see their faces filled with peace and joy. They learn from monks without even speaking to them. People do not see God in a monk who is loud, upset or aggressive. Be calm and a source of peace to others.

Monks who lose their inner peace become agitated and restless. They cannot stay in their cells, and are constantly moving around. Their movements are not gentle. When St. Moses was restless St. Isizorus asked him to stay in his cell, however St Moses couldn't do this. Why? Because his heart was lacking peace, he was disturbed.

When people lose their inner peace, their body language reflects their restlessness. Some people walk slowly, while others walk very quickly. Inner disturbances create feelings of discomfort and violent movements.

People can determine whether or not they are calm when they are exposed to a stressful situation. Those who stand firm and are not shaken in the face of tribulation are truly calm. We must not deceive ourselves and think that we are calm when we escape from problems. Anyone can be calm in the absence of problems.

Consider Joseph the Righteous; his brothers devised an evil conspiracy against him. They threw him into a well and falsely accused him. Can you imagine going through more problems than what he encountered? Yet Joseph still maintained his peace while he was in prison.

Another great example is the Virgin St. Mary. For the first and last time in the history of humanity a virgin became pregnant, unbelievable! What would people say about her, especially since she vowed to live a life of virginity? Yet St. Mary remained calm and silently accepted God's will. She did not even discuss it with her fiancé. She was neither disturbed nor frustrated.

Abraham, the father of many nations, was asked to offer his only son as a sacrifice. Remember, he waited for a son for many years and so it must have seemed like a very strange and difficult request. Yet, he was not disturbed.

Only strong hearts are filled with peace in the midst of trouble. They can be likened to rocks that are unaffected by the crashing waves of the ocean, or like a house built on a rock which never falls in the face of a storm. They are confronted by big problems but their heart is stronger. Thus a calm person is he who accepts problems and quietly solves them without being disturbed. However if one was to lose his peace, his problems will get worse.

Imagine the Israelites standing in front of the Red Sea with Pharaoh behind them. Moses could have easily lost his peace, but he did not. Why? Because he had faith. If he had lost his peace, he would have thought that there was no solution for the problem, that God had forsaken him. He would have sought human resources and failed.

Those who maintain their inner peace never feel troubled or disturbed when they face tribulations. They calmly solve any problem with faith, wisdom, patience, prayer and fasting. After all, worrying will not solve the problem, but can actually make it worse.

Calm people are strong because they have tolerance. Those who are easily angered or disturbed are weak. This is why St. Paul says, "We then who are strong ought to bear with the scruples of the weak, and not to please ourselves." (Rom 15:1). Those who lose their inner peace also lose their faith. He who believes that God is always loving and will intervene to solve the problem, will never lose his peace.

He who loses his inner peace also loses the work of the Holy Spirit in his heart, because the fruit of the Spirit is love, joy and peace. Some people are more naturally calm and peaceful, whereas others struggle and acquire it by overcoming themselves. For example, St Moses the Black was not naturally calm but had to struggle to achieve calmness and a peaceful nature.

Try to overcome yourself and gain humility through difficult exercises. Pray and ask the Lord to grant you peace and calmness. Our Lord Jesus Christ was very calm and humble as He said, "Learn from Me, for I am gentle and lowly in heart." (Matt 11:29). He taught us humility, "Tell the daughter of Zion, 'Behold, your King is coming to you, lowly, and sitting on a donkey, a colt, the foal of a donkey.'" (Matt 21:5).

The Lord was very calm when he was solving problems and dealing with the mistakes of others. Consider how he dealt with the Scribes and Pharisees. Although He was harshly criticised, accused and interrogated about His doctrine and spirituality, He remained calm as seen in the passage, "Then the Jews answered and said to Him, 'Do we not say rightly that

You are a Samaritan and have a demon?'" (John 8:48).
How did the Lord answer them? What did He say?
Nothing. They also said, "This fellow does not cast out
demons except by Beelzebub, the ruler of the demons."
(Matt 12:24). The Lord does not cast out demons except
by Beelzebub. Beelzebub? Is He working with the devil?
Yet, the Lord silently accepted their accusation and
wisely answered them. He did not say, "How could
you accuse Me of such a thing?" He did not order fire to
come down from Heaven and consume them. Instead,
He calmly said to them, "Every kingdom divided
against itself is brought to desolation, and every city
or house divided against itself will not stand. If Satan
casts out Satan, he is divided against himself. How
then will his kingdom stand? And if I cast out demons
by Beelzebub, by whom do your sons cast them out?"
(Matt 12:25-27). He answered them calmly with wise
words. He did not react in anger or frustration. He said
to them, "If I cast out demons by Beelzebub, by whom
do your sons cast them out?" That is, do the sons of the
Jews cast out demons through Beelzebub?

The Lord was accused of breaking the Law and the
Sabbath, yet He never responded in anger. Rather, He
calmly explained to His accusers that people could do
good things on the Sabbath.

The Lord was accused of many other things, yet He always answered in a calm and wise manner, without raising His voice.

May we all try to follow the example of the saints and maintain our inner peace. May we learn how to accept insults, deal with others and manage problems in a calm and peaceful manner. Inner peace is a distinguishing feature of a spiritual person.

Questions & Answers

A monk who wants to live comfortably according to his desires cannot be a martyr. Only those who crucify themselves totally can be martyrs as St. Paul the Apostle says, "I have been crucified with Christ; it is no longer I who live, but Christ lives in me." (Gal 2: 20). If a monk wants to live a life of martyrdom he has to crucify himself, "For whoever desires to save his life will lose it, but whoever loses his life for My sake and the gospel's will save it." (Mark 8: 35).

Some people say that the greatest virtue is asceticism, while others say it is prayer or silence. Is it then just a matter of monastic schools?

The aim of the monastic life is centred around God's love. The love of God is the main focus of our entire life and thus a monk practises virtues such as silence and asceticism as a means to achieve this goal.

If fasting, silence, and prayer do not lead to the love of God, then it is in vain. The ultimate target of our early fathers was the love of God. As a result of this love of God, a person is inwardly silent. Silence with a mind not focused on God is superficial. Our early fathers said, "Silence your tongue so that your heart may speak, and silence your heart so that God may speak."

Someone once asked one of the fathers, "Why don't you sit with us? Don't you like us?" He then answered, "God knows how much I love you, but I cannot talk to God and people at the same time."

If prayer is void of love it is not prayer. We pray to God because we love Him so much, "Oh, how I love Your law! It is my meditation all the day." (Ps.119: 97), "As the deer pants for the water brooks, so pants my soul for You, O God." (Ps. 42: 1). People talk to God in different ways out of their love for Him.

If silence, serenity or service leads you to the love of God that is great. It is important to live in the love of God and that is our aim in monasticism. One wants to live in solitude because of the love of God, not because of the glory, fame, or dignity of solitude. We live in silence because of the love of God, not because the saints were silent.

As far as I know about the essence and depth of monasticism, I believe that it was the love of God that compelled people to join a monastery more than the love of family, relatives, friends, service and the desire for marriage.

Can a person live as a monk amidst responsibilities?

In my opinion, the greatest examples in this field are Paul the Apostle and David the Prophet. I do not think that anyone of us has the same responsibilities as David the Prophet. He was a king for a country, and at that time the king was responsible for everything. He did not have many ministers to share his responsibility. He was also the army general and the judge for the people. At the same time he had a big family of at least eight wives and many children. He was living in an era full of problems, yet his heart was clinging to God day and night: "Oh, how I love Your law! It is my meditation all the day." (Ps.119: 97), "Seven times a day I praise You, because of Your righteous judgments." (Ps. 119: 164), "Evening, morning and noon...", "When I remember You on my bed, I meditate on You in the night watches." (Ps. 63: 6), "At midnight I will rise to give thanks to You, because of Your righteous judgments." (Ps.119: 62), "My eyes are awake through the night watches, that I may meditate on Your word." (Ps.119: 148) and "O God, You are my God; Early will I seek You; My soul thirsts for You;" (Ps. 63: 1), "When shall I come and appear before God?" (Ps. 42: 1-2).

Any person who is hindered by his responsibilities should remember David the Prophet.

None of us have toiled in service and teaching like St. Paul the Apostle. He even said: "but I laboured more abundantly than they all" (1 Cor.15: 10), "...in journeys often, in perils of water..." (2 Cor.11: 26); yet he was able to ascend to the third heaven and heard inexpressible words, which is not lawful for a man to utter.

There is an advice which I address to whoever has a responsibility, whether inside or outside the monastery and it would be good if we are able to fulfil it: practise prayers during work, even in a simple way and prayer will grow gradually. Mix your work with prayers and pray while you are walking alone or among people. I know it is hard because we can pray better when we are in our cells, but it is very important if a person can continually pray.

Joshua the son of Nun is another good example of a person who balanced prayer with responsibility. He was the army general to succeed Moses. He was bearing all of Moses' responsibilities and God told him, "This book of the Law shall not depart from your mouth, but you shall meditate in it day and night." Is this possible amidst all the responsibilities of Joshua? If it were not, then God would have not ordered it.

It is important that an individual trains himself during work, because if one does this his work will become blessed.

The second advice: "Be faithful over a few things, I will make you ruler over many things." (Matt 21:23). Be faithful in the few minutes when you pray and God will give you continuous prayer. You might be locking yourself in your cell but cannot pray because you have not practised praying outside your cell. Many monks sit in their cells but are always fought with three things: boredom, thoughts, and sleep. They may also waste their time in things like cleaning, organising their cell or worldly reading. St. Isaac says, "There is a monk who may spend 50 years sitting in his cell without knowing how to spend his time inside it."

Be faithful unto death, even if it leads you to martyrdom.

Some readings may cause more harm than good, such as reading about the fierce wars experienced in the lives of the saints. How can we avoid being negatively affected by these wars?

You should not dwell too much on the wars encountered by the saints, but rather focus on their victories. If these attacks are written in a way which may make you stumble, stay away from them. Some may read these attacks and would not be bothered by them. If you are affected by these words in a harmful way, you should use wisdom to discern what will help or harm you in your spiritual life.

We should have a positive spiritual work so that spiritual matters will be prioritised over worldly matters. Therefore whenever our mind goes astray, it will wonder in spiritual issues. How could we fight the thoughts if our mind is not occupied with spirituality?

St. John the Short kept repeating to himself, "the baskets for the camel man" so that he could remember to give the baskets to the camel man. His mind was always occupied with spiritual matters.

Let the spiritual thinking be dominant in your mind. It is better to substitute a worldly desire or thought with a spiritual one. Let your desire be on God's love instead of a sinful desire. This might take a while but it is definitely successful in the long term.

The difference between a working monk and an idle monk is this: a working monk has started gaining virtues and is storing for the unfruitful years that might attack him later, like Joseph when he stored the wheat in the land of Egypt. You should do the same, store spiritual thoughts to take over your mind when it goes astray. Try to correct any thought that is bothering you, otherwise it will keep attacking you.

A sick person will never be healed if he keeps taking painkillers. He needs to cure the disease itself. Choose to filter the harmful thoughts inside your mind and have peace with others regardless of the circumstances.

The harmful thought might be stored in your subconscious mind and press on you every now and then, thus you need to filter and remove the harmful thought.

I remember that in the early months of my monasticism, I used to dream and remember myself as a layman in a meeting or at church. However gradually with time, the picture of myself as a monk overtook my dreams and filled my subconscious mind.

It may happen that the attacks do not originate from you or from other people, but rather the devil. The solution is to concentrate your mind and feelings in prayers. Do not engage these thoughts but rather dismiss them and keep praying. A common statement that comes to mind is, "I have fights which disappear as soon as I finish praying". This means that the devil is launching fights to hinder you from praying.

This is why we pray in the Psalm, "Praise the LORD, O Jerusalem! Praise your God, O Zion! For He has strengthened the bars of your gates; He has blessed your children within you." (Ps. 147: 12, 13). Strengthening the bars of our gates means the bars of the thoughts. The hearing and the mind are closed to any harmful external thought. The Lord has blessed us with the work of the Holy Spirit within us to fight off these harmful thoughts.

In Song of Songs 4:1 we pray, "A garden enclosed is my sister, my spouse, a spring shut up, a fountain sealed" through which the small foxes destroying the vines cannot go. It is a garden enclosed against any outer war and it never opens its doors to anyone of God's enemies or anything hindering one's spiritual progress.

There are some jobs in the monastery which tire the mind such as the gatekeeper (the monk appointed to be the one who interacts with the public) of the monastery. How could this monk pray without straying or experiencing interruptions?

Every job has its responsibilities which might hinder one's ability to pray continuously. Most likely the porter will have long periods of free time if there are few visitors to the monastery. Thus during this time he could occupy himself with a spiritual work. However when visitors are present, he needs to meet them and accompany them inside with politeness and courtesy. He cannot tell people to wait outside until he finishes his spiritual work. There is a time for everything: a time for your duties and a time for prayers. The gatekeeper who reads and prays much will be able to preserve his mind when meeting visitors.

We should try to avoid the large crowd around the entrance to the monastery as some visitors spend too much time talking unnecessarily. Thus the gatekeeper should quickly lead the visitors to the monk responsible for them. It would be great if this monk could explain to the visitor's information about the monastery in a spiritual manner. This is the difference between an archaeologist and a monk. The archaeologist explains the information in a purely scientific way, while the monk explains the information in both a scientific and spiritual way.

A monk is asking: What should we do with a monk who is interfering in other monks' business?

Try talking to this monk about a different subject, and if he starts by saying, "Did you know that father so and so did so and so...." tell him, "This reminds me of a story in the 'Paradise of the Monks'. If you do so then you have succeeded.

How would a monk not lose the true value of Holy Communion even though he takes it daily?

Actually I do not feel comfortable when monks take holy communion daily because then it can turn into a habit. The monk loses readiness for communion. He may even approach communion even if he has an unresolved problem with another monk the previous day. Here communion just becomes a routine.

If there is spiritual growth in eternity, that means those who have reached the Kingdom were not perfect. How would there be growth while there is no sin in eternity? Are there any biblical references for this?

Of course absolute perfection is only for God. No matter how perfect people are on earth, it is only partial and incomplete. Thus there is also spiritual growth in heaven.

As for any biblical references, let us look at the example of St. Paul the apostle. He ascended to the third heaven and saw unutterable things. He saw visions and toiled more than all the other apostles, yet he said, "Not that I have already attained, or am already perfected; but I press on, that I may lay hold of that for which Christ Jesus has also laid hold of me. Brethren, I do not count myself to have apprehended; but one thing I do, forgetting those things which are behind and reaching forward to those things which are ahead, I press toward the goal for the prize of the upward call of God in Christ Jesus." (Phil. 3: 12-13). He forgot those perfect things he had reached, and looked forward to things ahead.

Then he added, "Therefore let us, as many as are mature, have this mind." (Phil 3: 15). This means, let us all look forward to develop in perfection.

Let us use an analogy to describe perfection. Say a child in year one who is studying mathematics learns addition and he achieves perfection in this area. At this stage his perfection of mathematics is limited only to addition at a year one level. In year two he excels in multiplication and division, but again is limited at a year two level where is still so much more to know. This progress continues on and on. He keeps progressing from one level to the other. This is why St. Paul says, "Therefore let us, as many as are mature, have this mind." meaning the mature should keep looking ahead. In heaven there is development from perfection to another, without limitations. Do you think that a person can reach a level of perfection on earth without any more potential for growth? It does not make sense that in heaven a person will just stop at whatever level of perfection he has reached while on earth.

Thus what is the use of being released from the earthly body and transformed into a spiritual body if he is not developing and benefiting from the new nature and the crown of righteousness?

In eternity the soul will have unlimited capabilities. It will always keep growing in knowledge of the Lord until it reaches higher levels of perfection.

How would development occur in eternity while there is no sin?

A person developing in love, knowledge, getting closer to God and enjoying His presence has nothing to do with sin. There are so many issues for development that are unrelated to any negative issues.

Do evil people also develop in eternity?

No. The evil ones are in the outer darkness and cannot develop perfection.

Elijah the Prophet appeared with the Lord on the Mount of Transfiguration in a glorified body. We know that at the end of days he will come back and die. How can a glorified body die?

Elijah did not have a glorified body yet. The glorified body is a state after the resurrection. His appearance with the Lord does not mean that He was in a glorified body. This reminds me of Moses when he spent 40 days with the Lord on the mountain and his face was illuminating. Thus the people asked him to wear a veil so that they could look at him, yet we cannot say that Moses had a glorified body because Moses died and glorified bodies are immortal. Thus Elijah did not have a glorified body. Sometimes the Lord grants light to people for a certain time only, but it is not a change of human nature. Change of human nature will be in the general resurrection, and this has not happened yet.

How can a person crucify himself?

To resist all his desires which pull him far away from God. To crucify every void word that does not build up. To crucify every wrong thought that is not according to monasticism. People in the world who have a pure mind stay away from sinful thoughts. As for a monk, in addition to staying away from sinful thoughts, he has to stay away from trifle thoughts and nonsense of the world, as these do not correspond with his monastic rules. A monk, who crucifies his thoughts and desires lives in a state of inner rational and spiritual martyrdom. He dies to every worldly desire which hinders the path to Christian perfection.

Toiling is also a factor in this struggle. St. John the Short was asked once, "what is monasticism? He answered, "it is toiling for the sake of God."

Those who toil for the sake of God find rest in Him. Everyone will be rewarded according to his struggle as written in St. Paul's first Epistle to the Corinthians, chapter 3. Some struggles include: pushing your body to wake up early for prayers, having reverence, keeping vigils, fasting with wisdom and guidance, restraining the body if it desires any luxurious food, living in silence, and staying away from human comfort being satisfied only with divine comfort. A monk should push himself in all of these struggles.

There is an important remark concerning the appropriate struggle for a monk and the narrow gate he should go through. The aforementioned is for novices.

A novice monk should push himself and crucify his desires in order to experience joy and happiness. He then would crucify would his mind, will and tongue, as they become easier matters to practice. The narrow gate is like a bottle neck which opens wide after moving through the narrow part, as mentioned in the verse, "He also brought me out into a broad place." (Ps. 18: 19). A monk would enjoy the joy of the resurrection after the first martyrdom and the crucifying of his worldly thoughts and desires.

How would a person crucify his worldly thoughts?

He should not accept a sinful or void thought through two ways:

1. Dismissing the thought and not yielding to it. This is a voluntary choice.

2. Being continuously busy with spiritual work in order to not give the worldly thoughts any chance to develop. This is what we call a protective action. The fighting of the worldly thoughts is easier for a monk who is busy with spiritual work.

Do not yield to the worldly thoughts even if it is just out of curiosity. Curiosity may lead to harmful results for the monk. The best thing is to dismiss the thought immediately in order to be strong, but if you negotiate with the thought it will overtake you and become harder to dismiss.

Sinful thoughts are extensive and not limited to adultery or pride. They may also include taking revenge or daydreaming. It is important that a monk be very disciplined with his thoughts.

What about the worldly thoughts which press a monk greatly. No matter how hard he is trying to remove these thoughts through prayers and prostrations, they are still attacking him?

A monk should not grieve when he has these thoughts because many of the saints had similar fights. St. Moses the Black went to his confession father St. Isidore eleven times in the same night. His father advised him to stay in his cell, but he could not. After a while the Lord comforted him from these worldly thoughts. St. Isaac says very comforting words about this situation, "it is not only the soldiers who have won the battle that are crowned and receive medals. It is also those who are steadfast in the war with wounded and broken bodies, that did not flee from the enemy but rather resisted him. They are also crowned and receive medals."

A thought might attack a person and he dismisses it without any damage done. Another person might resist the thought and be wounded, yet he is also crowned because of his struggle and fight.

St. Basil the Great says, "things that are easily won are easily lost. The Lord often postpones rescue in specific wars for a person so that he may fall and understand his weakness"

God responds to our prayers according to His plan for us. Sometimes God responds quickly but at other times we feel He takes longer in order to grant us patience and humility of heart. His 'delayed' response may occur so that we might have pity on others who are fighting similar wars as mentioned, "Remember the prisoners as if chained with them—those who are mistreated—since you yourselves are in the body also." {Heb.13: 3}

When St. Isaac talked about the spiritual guide, he said, "those who have fallen and risen up." This means that when a person falls and rises he will gain experience and have pity on others who are going through similar wars.

There is a story in "The Paradise of the Monks" about a monk who told an elder monk about his wars, and the latter said, "You will not be able to continue in monasticism, go back to the world." While he was leaving the monastery this monk met another elder monk who comforted and encouraged him so that he returned to the wilderness. This elder monk also asked God to let the other elder monk experience these wars of the young monk so that he might feel the pains people are suffering from. It happened that he could not tolerate even one day of these wars. Then the elder monk said to him, "it is because you had thrown the young monk into despair while he was struggling with the wars of the enemy." Sometimes God allows wars for us so that we might have pity on others. No matter how little others are falling, we all know the strength of the enemy as we say in our prayers, "O Lord, You know the vigilance of my enemies, and the weakness of my soul You understand, O my creator."

How can we differentiate between the thoughts coming from within ourselves and those coming from the devil?

You might enjoy the thoughts which are coming from within yourself, because you are the one who is thinking of them and like them to continue. As for the thoughts which are coming from the devil, you must reject them and remove them from all your heart, no matter how pressing they are. These thoughts can include blasphemy and doubts. They can fight a faithful heart as they are coming from the devil.

Thoughts might also come as a result of laxity and a failure to control the senses. If you read, hear, or see inappropriate things, this will bring inappropriate thoughts. Inappropriate reading can especially have a negative impact. Be very disciplined with what you read.

The hardest thing is when you cannot discern if the thoughts are coming from God, the devil or yourself. If the thoughts are from God, they will bring relief and make you feel comfortable. As for the thoughts that are clearly sinful stay away from them.

There can be harmful thoughts which come as a result of reading the sayings of the fathers or reading in general. How can we address this?

You should always have discernment in what you read, even in the sayings of the fathers and the verses of the Holy Bible. Misunderstanding can cause harm, thus you should have guidance concerning these matters. The sayings of the fathers and their lives are not suitable for everyone. They lived in a certain era, with different circumstances. Imitating the fathers without discernment or consultation is very dangerous.

Therefore we need to:

1. Correctly understand the sayings of the fathers.

2. Understand that not everything we read is suitable to be applied.

How can we address evil and its relationship to God in light of the verse "I make peace and create calamity; I, the Lord, do all these things" (Isa 45:7)?

In order to understand the Holy Bible, we have to understand when there is symbolic meaning. The word 'evil' in the Holy Bible bears two meanings; 'sin' and 'hardship or calamity'. This is clear in Job the Righteous' words, "Shall we indeed accept good from God, and shall we not accept adversity (evil)?" He did not mean 'sin' when saying 'adversity', but he meant the difficulty of losing his children and possessions.

It is written, "many evils and troubles shall befall them." (Deut.31: 17). Here the word evil does not mean 'sin' but it means 'difficulties'.

When God talked to Josiah the King about captivity, He said, "Surely, therefore, I will gather you to your fathers, and you shall be gathered to your grave in peace; and your eyes shall not see all the calamity which I will bring on this place." (2 Kings 22: 20). Here the calamity is not sin but the captivity.

Thus, the word peace and calamity means that both difficulties and grace come from God.

What does it mean 'make friends for yourselves by unrighteous mammon' (Luke 16:9)?

By saying 'unrighteous mammon' He did not mean the money gained through sin because the Lord forbids any sinful means for gaining a virtue. The Psalm says "It shall be as excellent oil; Let my head not refuse it." (Ps. 141: 5). God even refused the offerings from evil people, "You shall not bring the wages of a harlot or the price of a dog to the house of the Lord your God for any vowed offering, for both of these are an abomination to the Lord your God." (Deut.23: 18). The church never accepts donations that come as a result of corruption.

What does 'unrighteous mammon' mean then? It does not mean money coming from unjust deeds and then using it for good deeds, for God disapproves of this. It means that when you are asked to give tithes and the first fruits of your income to the needy or the church and fail to do so, that means you are being unjust towards God, the church and the needy. It is written, "Will a man rob God? Yet you have robbed Me! But you say, 'In what way have we robbed You?' In tithes and offerings." (Mal 3: 8). It means you have robbed God and did not give Him His share. You have been unjust to the needy and the church.

If you have been unjust and kept this money in your pocket, try to make friends by giving that money to the church and the needy because they will pray for you and intercede on your behalf. The rich are not necessarily unjust people, but they are unjust if they love money and refuse to give it to the church and the needy.

We have to go beyond just the level of tithing and offering first fruits as these are Old Testament commandments representing the minimum we should offer. It is written in the New Testament, "Give to him who asks you, and from him who wants to borrow from you do not turn away." (Matt.5: 42). You are unjust if you do not give him, because you already have. There is a very important verse about this matter, "Whoever shuts his ears to the cry of the poor will also cry himself and not be heard." (Prov. 21: 13).

What do we know about the devil?

The devil is an angel who has lost his purity, but kept his nature and power as described in the story of Job. He has an astonishing power to even destroy houses and create winds. Also in second Thessalonians

Chapter 2, it mentions "The coming of the lawless one according to the working of Satan, with all power, signs, and lying wonders." Some people will believe him causing the falling away, and that is through the power of the devil.

It is written in the Holy Bible that at the end times the devil will be released and mislead many that "unless those days were shortened, no flesh would be saved; but for the elect's sake those days will be shortened." (Matt.24: 22).

Thus the devil is still powerful because he did not lose his angelic nature. It is written, "Bless the Lord, you His angels, who excel in strength." (Ps. 103: 19). He has great strength, power, wisdom and intelligence – of course it is an evil wisdom, "Now the serpent was more cunning than any beast of the field which the Lord God had made." (Gen.3: 1). St. Paul also says, "for we are not ignorant of his devices." (2 Cor.2: 11).

The devil is resilient and will keep resisting until he is thrown in the lake of fire and brimstone. It was said about Judas Iscariot "Now after the piece of bread, Satan entered him". Also, "Peter took Him aside and began to rebuke Him, saying, "Far be it from You, Lord; this shall not happen to You!" But He turned and said to Peter, "Get behind Me, Satan! You are an offense to

Me." (Matt.16: 23). This shows that the devil can inspire a person with an evil idea.

Some theologians said that the statement "If You are the Son of God, come down from the cross" is one of the statements Satan made to Jesus, exactly like, "If You are the Son of God, command that these stones become bread." (Matt.4: 3).

The story of the fall of Satan is written in Isaiah 14. Jesus also said "I saw Satan fall like lightning from heaven". He wanted to be like God, "I will exalt my throne above the stars of God....I will be like the Most High."

How does the devil perform work even though he is tied up in the pit?

The devil is tied up by God, and does not have full freedom as he did previously. This does not mean that he is not working. He is working but not with full freedom, and after his release he will work more freely. We might ask, 'since he is tied up how can so much evil exist around the world?' I am telling you, believe me, if he has total freedom no one would be living in peace. This is why the Lord said, "And unless those days were shortened, no flesh would be saved; but for the elect's sake those days will be shortened." (Matt.24: 22).

We can see the freedom of the devil in Sodom and Gomorrah before the flood and when the entire world perished except for only eight people. There was even a time when only one person was worshipping God, while the entire world was worshipping idols. This occurred when the children of Israel worshipped the golden calf while Moses was on the Mountain. Only Moses worshipped God, while the people of Israel, including Aaron the chief priest who made the golden calf, worshipped idols.

These events reveal to us the power of the devil. His power will be seen very clearly when the falling away will take place. He will perform wonders and miracles through the Anti-Christ, but in the end he will perish with a blow from Christ's mouth.

www.ingramcontent.com/pod-product-compliance
Lightning Source LLC
Chambersburg PA
CBHW022119080426
42734CB00006B/187